Joseph and Lucy Smith's Tunbridge Farm: An Archaeology and Landscape Study

Mark L. Staker and Donald L. Enders

John Whitmer Books
Independence, Missouri
2021

© 2021 BY THE JOHN WHITMER HISTORICAL ASSOCIATION

Published by John Whitmer Books
John Whitmer Books is a trademark of the John Whitmer Historical Association

ISBN 978-1-934901-21-2

Learn more about the John Whitmer Books and the John Whitmer Historical Association at www.JWHA.info

PRINTED IN THE UNITED STATES OF AMERICA

Table of Contents

Introduction 1

Chapter One: Tunbridge Gore 4

Chapter Two: Asael Smith's First Land Purchase 7

Chapter Three: The Smith Farm 11

Chapter Four: The Smith Log Cabin 23

Chapter Five: Smith Family Comforts of Life 35

Chapter Six: A Smith Industrial Building 44

Chapter Seven: Selling Smith Settlement 48

Chapter Eight: Lucy's Meadow, Her Grove, and Her First Vision 56

Notes 71

Index 111

About the Authors 113

Acknowledgements

We are indebted to Scott and Patricia Beavers who own Ward Hill Meadow where the Smith home once stood. We cannot overstate their contribution to this project, as they gave access to their property and allowed us to excavate the home site. We are also grateful to the Publication Services Division of the Church of Jesus Christ of Latter-day Saints Church History Department for two research grants that helped fund part of this project. Bob Dunkle, who operates an Airbnb on Spring Road in Tunbridge, Vermont, also generously helped our project. Most of the research, however, was funded through frequent flyer miles, vacation days, and personal funds.

We are also indebted to Joe Mendor, senior facilities manager at the Joseph Smith Birthplace, who lent us tools for the dig. Dawn Adeyemi received and mailed equipment and artifacts on our behalf at the Joseph Smith Birthplace. Euclid Farnham, Tunbridge town historian, Ben Wolfe, Tunbridge librarian, and Paul Harwood, Harwood Forestry Services, all provided insights and served as a sounding board. Many other Tunbridge citizens in the town clerk's office, general store, and elsewhere shared their knowledge, let us look at their early homes, or contributed in other ways. Our project was a community effort. The residents of Ward Hill were particularly generous with their memories of the surrounding area. In addition to Scott and Patricia Beavers, those who helped us were Ray and Beverly Young, Evelyn Sargant, and Fred Green. They treated us flatlanders like hill people.

Many Church Service Missionaries working at the Joseph Smith Birthplace of the Church of Jesus Christ of Latter-day Saints gave up their shopping day. And members of the Montpelier Stake, especially the South Royalton Ward, volunteered their time. They all worked hot days covered in dirt from crown to foot helping dig the site. Two families of tourists also stopped during their vacation and helped for a few hours. Lloyd L. Caswell of the South Royalton Ward helped for many days on the project by painstakingly scraping dirt inside the west foundation wall inch by inch for long, tedious hours.

Lindsay Johansson, from the University of Colorado, Boulder, donated her time to help with the osteology, and Ryan Saltzgiver, from the Church of Jesus Christ of Latter-day Saints Church History Department helped facilitate the osteology work. Tom Visser, director of the Historic Preservation Program at the University of Vermont, shared his own results at neighboring archaeology sites, as we worked to date periods of historic nails in Vermont. Matthew Kirk, Hartgen Archaeological Associates, volunteered the expertise on dating of some artifacts. Ezekiel (Zeke) Goodband, the apple grower at Scott Farm in Dummerston, Vermont, and one of the leading apple growers in the United States, volunteered his time to identify Smith family apple varieties. Anne Berryhill in the Church History Library in Salt Lake City assisted in getting permission to publish photographs. And Jenny Lund, Director of the Historic Sites Division of The Church of Jesus Christ of Latter-day Saints, gave encouragement and advice. Finally, this project could never have been done without the generous support and dedicated efforts of Scott Esplin, Reed Russell, Cheryle Grinter, Daniel Stone, and Carmen Cole, who shepherded this book through the publishing process at John Whitmer Books.

Introduction

Asael and Mary Duty Smith left their rented dairy farm in Ipswich, Massachusetts, sometime in October 1791 for the woods of Tunbridge Mountain in Vermont. After they arrived, they cleared the land and tried to make a living in the rocky hills of the Green Mountains for almost twenty years. As their older children married, divided the property, or purchased adjacent lots for farms where they could raise their own families, a small community grew around them that their neighbors called "Smith Settlement."[1] Here a son, Joseph, married Lucy Mack, who was born and raised in the mountain culture of New Hampshire. They settled near family on a 43-acre farm divided from the original purchase. It included a small meadow and almost forty acres of "mountains"—hills really—where they briefly tried agriculture. The granite hills were worn down by centuries of forests on their surface and included large quartz stones that made shiny, decorative foundation stones for a comfortable home.[2] Lucy brought her mountain worldview into their marriage, as she and Joseph started a family and chose an economic direction that changed the trajectory of their family's history.[3] Drought, cold, and economic fluctuations drove many people out of Vermont, including the Smith family, and over time Smith Settlement disappeared from the landscape. As Vermonter Stewart Holbrook watched this happen to his own mountain community while a young boy, it had such an impact on him he wrote as an adult about seeing "old cellar holes" everywhere and reminisced how "the orchards being slowly throttled by encroaching forest moved me deeply. I had a fairly good idea of what had gone into the making of those hill farms and homes; and the fact they had been abandoned . . . seemed to me a great tragedy. It still does."⁴ His own family arrived in the mountains during the same wave of immigration that brought Asael and Mary Smith and thousands of others, but the Smiths left sooner. Nature's push back, however, eventually drove Holbrook's family from their hill farm as well and into a village. Holbrook watched as

> the entire hill was enveloped with the immense hush of an illimitable wilderness. . . . the silence is returning, along with the wilderness that is marching from the edges of the old fields and pastures straight across and up and down, swallowing the miles of stone fences, tearing the pasture gate off its hinges, advancing to the barn to break its ribs, and arriving, at last, at the very slab of granite that served as a doorstep, while the house itself, with a few decaying apple trees and a bush of lavender, is about to be crushed, then wholly obliterated, along with the rest of a typical hill farm of the Green Mountain State.⁵

When this happened to Smith Settlement, as nature devoured the main structures and then swallowed the remaining garbage scattered around them from the first married homestead of Joseph and Lucy Smith, it left behind little but the gaping cellar hole from the original home and a few scattered apple trees marking the place of a once productive orchard. But the site still has a story to tell of Joseph and Lucy Smith's early history together and their struggle to establish a family on their Tunbridge Mountain farm.

To learn more about this pivotal period in Smith family history, we did archaeology at the original homesite during October 25–30, 2016 and August 6–19, 2017.⁶ A team of dedicated volunteers helped us with critical aspects of this effort.⁷ We also made a careful study of the physical setting of the Smith family farm within the larger community.⁸ And we searched the surviving documents of the area to better understand the historical context. This monograph focuses on the physical context of the Joseph Smith Sr. and Lucy Mack Smith farm in Tunbridge, Vermont, sharing some insights that add to the larger narrative of their Vermont experience.

Volunteers Working at Dig Site
Unless otherwise credited, all maps, sketches, and photographs, including this one, were created by Mark Staker.

Chapter One
Tunbridge Gore

Smith Settlement was once a part of Royalton Township chartered by Governor George Clinton of New York in 1769. Clinton established the township with 30,000 acres of mountains in Windsor County, Vermont, that included all of what is still Royalton, plus parts of what are now Bethel, Barnard, and Sharon Townships in Windsor County, and the bottom of what is now Tunbridge Township in Orange County— including a remote area that later became known as Tunbridge Gore. He sold the Royalton property to investors for fourteen to eighteen shillings ($1.78–$2.29) an acre in New York currency.[1]

Elias Stevens, one of Clinton's initial investors, bought several tracts of the property and built a log home in a Royalton meadow. During the Revolutionary War, Lieutenant Richard Houghton of the British Army's 53rd Regiment led 300 Mohawk warriors down from Canada through central Vermont to carry out revenge attacks. Houghton was looking for Lieutenant Whitcomb, an American officer whose scouting party had come upon British General Gordon in the woods where they robbed and killed him.[2] Whitcomb lived in Newbury but Houghton and his men became lost and found themselves in nearby Tunbridge where they camped out on or by what would become Smith Settlement. Early the next morning, as a fog lifted off the First Branch of the White River on October 16, 1780, Houghton led a surprise attack on defenseless settlers living mostly along the river.

Stevens was in one of his fields loading a fall harvest of pumpkins when they arrived.[3] The Mohawks under Houghton's orders "made the Stevens meadow their rendezvous." And when Stevens' wife and children saw the heavily armed men in warpaint coming toward their isolated cabin they ran into the nearby woods.[4] David Waller ran to warn Elias Stevens. Waller was a fourteen-year-old boy living with the Stevens family whose older brother John would later marry Asael and Mary Smith's daughter Priscilla. Young Waller didn't make it to Stevens and the Mohawk captured him and made him a prisoner.[5] Others were not so fortunate. Houghton's men killed four settlers. Then they rounded up twenty-eight to thirty-two men, including Waller, and marched them to Montreal. Some of the captives died, but Waller returned to Royalton after the war to write about his experiences. The Mohawk never left an account from their perspective, but the local settlers left many accounts and retold their experiences regularly. Their accounts of what they called "the Royalton massacre" shaped the identity of their community. And their memory of those events shaped everything that happened in the region afterward.

Stevens and his family survived the raid. But their house was gone, and they felt vulnerable. They decided to sell their mountain property and concentrate their efforts on land down by the river closer to the village. Stevens worked with his friend Joel Marsh for more than a decade pushing several proposals to government committees hoping to resolve lingering boundary disputes between New York and New Hampshire.[6]

Solomon Gale later acknowledged when he surveyed the township northwest of Royalton in 1774 (he still called it Middlesex, its New York name, rather than Randolph, its New Hampshire name), that he made incorrect assumptions about the 1770 survey work of Thomas Valentine defining Royalton's boundaries. Gale fixed the southern boundary of Middlesex too far north of the Royalton line. This left a large strip of unsurveyed land between Royalton and what became the township to its north—Tunbridge. In New England, a section of land not part of any township is called a *gore*. So, Gale's survey mistake created a gore between Royalton and Tunbridge.[7]

One advantage of living in a gore at the end of the eighteenth century was that without a township to levy taxes, a family could live tax-free. For that reason, Experience Davis, a Presbyterian Deacon who would later become a potential spiritual advisor to Lucy Smith, cleared out a "Squatter lot" in Randolph Township on the ridge just west of Stevens property, and petitioned for a gore designation of the area between Royalton and Tunbridge on October 3, 1778. When he failed to get it, John Hutchinson and others petitioned for an official gore designation on February 5, 1780. Amid legal wrangling and the attempt by neighboring towns to get control over the area, on June 2, 1785, Elias Stevens and a neighbor, Silas Williams, petitioned on behalf of Royalton to have their initial boundaries reinstated to bring their property back into Royalton Township. Two weeks later, on June 18, 1785, the Vermont Assembly decided against their petition, then recognized Tunbridge Gore, and later that day assigned the land to Tunbridge Township.[8] Although it was now officially part of the township, residents of Tunbridge continued to refer to the area as a gore, and they levied some taxes—such as those to operate school districts—separate from those of the township government. When Asael Smith bought his first property in Tunbridge, it was already part of the township, but his deed referred to his new farm, as did many other deeds before and after, as a "Tract of Land lying and being in the gore betwens [sic] The Township of Royalton and Tunbridge."[9]

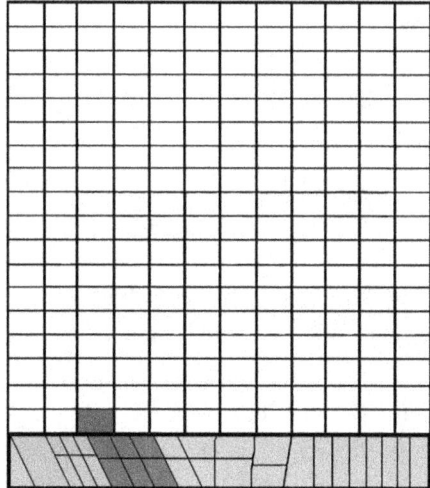

Smith Property and Lots in Tunbridge Township and Gore
Mark Staker, based on original town plat

Chapter Two
Asael Smith's First Land Purchase

Elias Stevens and the other original investors divided their land into smaller parcels and sold eighty-three to one-hundred-acre lots at a profit. The best sites sold as mill seats, pastures, and prime village locations. And the land in the valley extending to the west of the First Branch of the White River sold quickly to new settlers who came primarily from New Hampshire or Massachusetts. After the prime valley land sold, Stevens began selling his mountain property in the southwestern corner of the township. It was low quality farmland, and he sold two-hundred of his best acres in the gore for eight shillings an acre the year before Asael Smith arrived in Tunbridge.[1]

Since Stevens hired Israel and Anna Waller's son David to work for him, and Anna Waller was born and married in Topsfield, Massachusetts, she may have shared news of cheap land with friends there.[2] The woods Stevens offered for sale in the gore had few or no tax advantages. And it had little else to offer: its soil was thin, its ground rocky, and its location remote. A significant part of it was shaded by the hills of Tunbridge Mountain dotted with dramatic outcroppings of stone. Its rugged slopes were covered with thick hardwood forest. And its connection with a recent massacre made it even less attractive than land in other regions of the Green Mountains.

One of the least attractive features of Stevens's meadow for most farmers was its natural fen.[3] Water runs constantly underground through the meadow between two mountains keeping it wet year-round while growing high marsh grasses through the summer. Fens are too wet to grow grain or other principle crops well. They do not grow maple trees. But while most settlers would not want the land, this may have given the Smith family an advantage and attracted them to the site. They had generations of experience with fens.

When Robert Smith contracted as an indentured servant in 1638 to get passage to America, he did so in Lincolnshire, England, where 300,000 acres of fenland stretched southward into the countryside.[4] After Robert arrived in America, he worked on John Whittingham's coastal four-hundred-acre plantation in Massachusetts Bay Colony which included more than a hundred acres of fen filled with saltmarsh grass. Robert's son Samuel Sr. and grandson Samuel Jr. settled along the marshlands of Pye Brook in Topsfield, Massachusetts, and their property was mostly a fen between their house and the brook. Asael and some of his children, including Joseph Sr., were born and raised on that Topsfield fen, and Asael's son John remembered cutting saltmarsh grass as a major activity of his youth.[5] Asael Smith's Vermont farm replicated the same relationship between his childhood house on an embankment overlooking a fen in Topsfield, Massachusetts, and his new house on an embankment overlooking a fen in Tunbridge, Vermont.[6] When Joseph Smith Sr. later bought land in Manchester, New York, it included significant wetlands along Crooked Creek that offered similar growing conditions to a fen.[7]

While the Vermont and later New York properties did not grow saltmarsh grasses, they did grow cordgrass. In the Vermont wetlands cordgrass can grow to more than four feet tall, and dairymen today still prize it as hay for their livestock—especially cattle.[8] Perennial cordgrass produces more carbohydrates per square yard than wheat or barley with significantly less effort.[9]

Asael Smith may have seen the cordgrass growing along the lower spring and in the fenland of Stevens's meadow before he decided to buy the land. As he and Stevens got together to discuss a price, they did so in a time when almost everything was negotiable, and every transaction required some skill to arrange to advantage. Elias Stevens, elected Brigadier General of the Royalton militia just a few weeks after selling Smith his property, had a "commanding personality, strong voice, great will of force and mental power," although he was "not a professor of religion" and could press a hard bargain. But although six-feet tall and broad-shouldered, he was a little stooping.[10] Family tradition remembered Asael Smith as tall with a well-proportioned and powerful body "capable of handling with ease two ordinary men."[11] He liked to joke, had some political prowess in local governance and modest military experience as a Private, but tended to share his intense religious views to the point of annoying his neighbors. Smith had been badly burned as a child, and the scarring pulled at the side of his head, so his neighbors knew him as "Crook Necked Smith."[12]

No one specifically mentioned Smith's negotiating skills, but it is likely few others wanted the Stevens mountain property of two hillocks and a soggy meadow. The two large men agreed to a price of twenty-six pounds for lot 18 North. Smith paid six shillings three pence an acre for the 83-acre parcel.[13] This was almost twenty-five percent less than other land Stevens sold in the gore and significantly less than land that sold in the valley along the river. Since Stevens bought the land using New York Pounds, however, and Smith's property deed noted he paid in Vermont money—as the law required—Smith paid more per acre than a simple comparison of figures might suggest. Asael Smith needed £135 in Massachusetts notes to buy £100 in British sterling, while his £100 British sterling could buy £175 in New York notes.[14] But, Vermont currency officially traded at £100 British sterling for every £30 in Vermont notes.[15] And, Continental dollars traded at £100 British sterling for $444.44.[16] This exchange rate put Smith's purchase at an equivalent of $4.63 per acre, or $384.25 for the 83 acre lot—about double what Stevens paid for it when he bought it as part of a larger tract in New York money—but still a great price and easily paid for in New England's postwar growth economy.

Each acre of the Smith property cost a little more than a schoolteacher's weekly salary, officially set in Royalton at five shillings six pence. The town paid their local minister 20 shillings every Sunday, the equivalent of three of Smith's acres.[17] Because Asael Smith was a master cooper, and his sons were capable journeymen coopers able to do wet cooperage (making barrels that could hold liquid), they could easily earn more than a schoolteacher or a minister.[18] This allowed them to rapidly expand their holdings and prepare for the anticipated marriages of a family of seven boys, each needing his own household.

Asael also had to consider the contribution of the women of the household when he negotiated a price. John Smith recalled, "my mother was a first rate Dairy woman," and he remembered they had "considerable of a stock of cows."[19] Mary's four daughters—Priscilla, Mary (Polly), Susannah, and Sarah Smith—worked as dairymaids under their mother's direction. Since a typical good dairy herd had a little more than a dozen cows, they would each have responsibility for a couple of milkers.[20] When the Smiths bought their land, a dairy was "the unchallenged preserve of female authority and labor."[21] And the opinions of the Smith women would carry great weight.[22] A conservative estimate of the Smith women's earnings suggests they were bringing in at least three shillings a week through their dairy.[23] But they could have easily made double that.

Smith and Stevens negotiated to conclusion the land transaction on June 21, 1791, and with Joel Marsh as the Justice of the Peace they recorded it the following day. While twenty-two-year-old Jesse Smith was with his father and old enough to act as a witness, Marsh served as his own witness on the deed along with Royalton resident Heman Durkee.[24]

Chapter Three
The Smith Farm

Meadow

The features of the Smith 83-acre farm suggest its use. Its meadow is 1175 feet above sea level. West of the meadow a hill rises 120 feet; and east of the meadow a hill rises approximately 145 feet for an extended length with its highest point at the north reaching 153 feet above the meadow.[1] Today maple forest grows thickly on both hills. The meadow between the hills is watered by two springs. The lower spring flows into a brook that widens as it moves southward through the fen. Underground water joins it until the brook grows into a stream that rushes through a deep crevice it has cut near the southern boundary of the meadow.

A small hillock rises out of the wetlands at the south end of the meadow where trees grow in an old grove. Here early settlers created a cemetery to the west side of the stream. The wood grave markers in the cemetery have long since rotted away, and the earliest stone grave marker is that of Lucy and Joseph Smith's neighbor, Isaac Buck, who was buried on December 29, 1801.[2]

Natural Spring in Smith Meadow

The upper natural spring runs down the side of the west hill and is high enough it could provide running water through wood pipes to the Smith house—which later property deeds and physical evidence confirms occurred.[3] The spring was also ideally suited to run water in pipes down to a second spring in the meadow near the west hill. The second spring is much larger than the one on the hillside, and during the late nineteenth and the first part of the twentieth century the Young family living on Ward Hill kept a large basin in it to serve as a buttery.[4] A 1907 photograph of the homesite shows remnants of a stone foundation visible at the spring from an earlier building that stood over it (see page 32). The building remnants in the photograph appear to be those of a commercial size eighteenth-century buttery surrounding the spring. This would be typical for a large dairy but has not been investigated archaeologically.

The meadow is always wet south of the springs where water flows toward the cemetery. Sugar maples and most useful hardwoods can't grow there but it is well suited for growing cordgrass and other pasturage for cattle. North of the springs the meadow has about one acre where wild apple trees grow today. These apples are five different early varieties that could be descendants of trees planted by the Smiths. They grow fruit from two to three-inches in diameter.

Maiden Blush Apple in Smith Meadow

One of the apple varieties on the Smith property is the Bethel apple, named after neighboring Bethel Township. Joseph Smith Sr.'s sister Priscilla married into the Waller family that became prominent in Bethel. Her brother-in-law Daniel Waller built a brick hotel there.[5] This apple tree was widely grown in the county before the end of the eighteenth century. Its fruit keeps well during the winter months for extended fresh eating and pies.

Maiden Blush is another variety that grows in the meadow. It is considered one of the oldest American varieties of apples and was widely grown before the end of the eighteenth century. Maiden Blush apples ripen over an extended period during August and September and are therefore not a good commercial variety. But they are perfect for a family only able to process small batches at a time over an extended period. They make particularly good eating in pies and sauces.[6] After Joseph and Lucy Smith moved from their Tunbridge farm, their purchases from brother Jesse Smith's store included quarts of applesauce, suggesting it was an important part of the family diet.[7]

A third apple variety growing in the Smith meadow is the Yellow Belleflower.[8] This apple originated in New Jersey in 1742. The fruit is generally elongated and yellow with speckled brown and tinges of pink. Since it is a late-blooming apple that performs well in drought conditions, it does well in the colder climate of Vermont's Green Mountains with occasional late frosts. But nineteenth-century fruit growers also considered the Yellow Belleflower particularly well suited to the soil of Essex County, Massachusetts, where the Smith family lived before moving to Vermont.[9] Since it only stores well for a few months, the Smiths would have to eat them all before Christmas, cut them and dry them on a string, or turn them into cider. They were most likely processed into cider, along with the last two unidentified varieties. These have a bitter tinge that makes them particularly good for cider. But drought and frost during the period of study hampered identifying their variety—both weather complications that likely hampered Smith period production occasionally as well.

Smith Hills

The bulk of the Smith farm consists of its two hills, one on each side of the meadow. These hills were both dairy pasture within living memory, but for the past seventy years they have been growing timber.[10] Beneath the trees, however, there is still evidence of land use 200 years ago. The hillsides are lined with the remains of eighteenth-century stringer fences on the north and south property lines used to control cattle. These fences had a stone base with split rails on top; the stone designed to keep cattle from pushing through the fence and the rails to keep them from jumping over. Although the rails decayed long ago, the massive stones at the base, sometimes weighing two or three tons, still mark the fence line. To make these fences, Jesse and Joseph Smith, with the help of the younger Smith men, rolled massive stones onto a flat "stone boat," or large wooden sled, pulled by a team of oxen, and drug them to the fence line where they were rolled into place with the help of poles as levers. Fence construction was of necessity a family effort.[11]

The Smith fences do not continue strong to their end, but as they approach the eastern boundary line they get lower and narrower until they end as a few fist-sized rocks half buried in the ground. In the eighteenth century, these fences with the addition of wood rails on the top would have been approximately four feet high, but today they are approximately 24-inches high. The stone fence running along the south boundary of lot 18 North from the present road up the eastern hill goes for 360 feet, then it begins to get shorter in height continuing as a partial fence slowly descending to ground level and ending as a few scattered stones on the surface, for a total length of just over 564 feet.

On the northern boundary of lot 18 North, a stone fence approximately 30-inches high begins 82 feet from the west side of the road and runs east up to the road, continuing east for a total of 255 feet. The fence then turns northeast and runs from the joint of the turn another 631 feet 9 inches until it reaches lot 10 in Tunbridge proper where Asael and Mary Smith moved when they sold Joseph and Lucy Smith lot 18 North.[12]

Observing fencing carefully can offer clues to land use. Finding rocks (for early Vermonters these were much smaller than stones and easily moved by a single person) scattered along a fence line is a sign a field was once plowed rather than pasture.[13] These rocks rose to the surface each winter pushed up by the frost after the trees were felled and their roots began to decay. Where pastures quickly developed, the thick grass roots continued to hold most rocks underground. Where fields were plowed each year, the frost pushed up smaller fist-size rocks every spring and eventually even larger ones. Because these rocks rose underneath the snow, early settlers assumed the warming sun brought them to the surface in the spring.[14] These were gathered and tossed along the fence line to keep them out of the field.[15] Sometimes, when a lot of small rocks collected along a fence line, the early settlers worked them into the fence itself and fences with these smaller rocks stacked on top of the large stones are common.[16] Because the Smith fence does not have smaller rocks worked into it, and there are relatively few scattered along its base, this suggests the hills in lot 18 North were not plowed beyond what was needed to create pastureland.

Replica Stringer Fence, Eastfield Village, New York   *Stringer Fence Remains, Southeast Line Smith Farm*

Additional evidence the hills were used as pasture is found in the rough surface of the hillsides. When trees fall in the forest, the root ball pulls up leaving a hole in the ground. As the ball decays, it leaves a small hill of dirt beside the pit. These mounds and dips are called pillows and cradles. Pillows and cradles are essential features of all old growth forests.[17] Over centuries they cover the forest floor until the ground looks like the skin of an American toad. If a settler cleared trees and only plowed the ground a few times to let grass grow for a pasture, he would leave modest pillows and cradles behind but not as prominent features. If a settler continued to plow and harrow fields for crops every spring for years, he made the ground smooth.[18] The Smith hills have the slight undulations of a pasture instead of the smooth surface of regularly plowed land.

Jesse purchased lot 19 North just east of Asael and Mary's lot 18 North. On top of the east hill where his lot 19 joined Joseph Smith Sr.'s half of lot 18, the ground is level on Jesse's side of the boundary line from years of plowing and harrowing. The smooth land begins on the top of the hill where the stone fence line disappears, suggesting Jesse and Hannah Smith used worm fences that zigzagged along that boundary and could be moved around as land use changed.

Lightly Plowed Smith Hill

Immediately north and northwest of lot 18, Asael and Mary Smith purchased lot 10 in Tunbridge Township, just outside of the gore, where they moved and settled. It is largely hill free and is smooth from years of plowing and harrowing—even in some areas now thickly wooded with one- or two-hundred-year-old trees. The lack of pillows and cradles on the Asael and Mary Smith property may have been due to heavy plowing by later farmers. But it suggests they could have included some planting to accompany their dairy work.

Additional telling features on the landscape include the compact earth still visible in the maple forest where once well-worn cattle trails existed, and a massive stone outcropping in the center of the east hill bigger than a log cabin, a prominent feature after trees were cut down during the Smith Settlement period. Joseph, Lucy and their children would have seen the massive outcropping each morning as they went out their front door.[19]

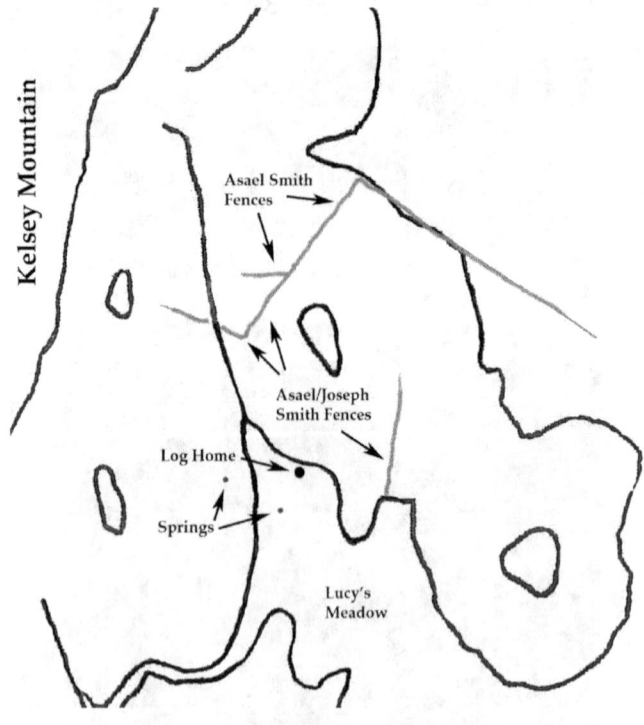

Smith Property Features
Map by Mark Staker

Because of lot 18 North's small meadow, well-placed springs, and dominant hills, it was well-suited as pasture for the "considerable" number of Smith cows. The hillsides could have supported any of the breeds of cattle available, but the soggy meadowlands with particularly soft ground around the water sources would have given way under the weight of larger breeds. Only small, productive Jersey cows could have used the Smith meadow.[20] This is the same breed of cows still raised in Tunbridge's mountains.

"Cultivating" the Land

When Lucy Smith shared with her scribe her first memories of moving to Smith Settlement, she said: "Having visited my father and mother [after her wedding], we returned again to Tunbridge, where my husband owned a handsome farm; which upon <which we> settled ourselves, upon it and began to cultivate the soil. We lived on this place about six years, tilling the earth for livlihood (sic)."[21] Her mention of cultivating and tilling when considered in light of the strong evidence for dairying not only suggests a major transition in land use when Lucy came to the farm but raises questions as to what she meant by cultivating since there is evidence their hills were not regularly plowed.

The evidence is mixed, and we don't yet have definitive answers, but there are some possibilities suggested by the landscape. Lucy grew up with tavern experience, and her sister Lydia Mack Bill, with whom she had a close relationship, inherited and ran a tavern with her husband Samuel Bill in Gilsum, New Hampshire.[22] Lucy's brother Stephen owned "a very large tavern" in Tunbridge.[23] It is possible Lucy was working in her brother's tavern when she met Joseph Smith.[24] Lucy continued to rely on her tavern experience for years after she left Vermont. When she first moved to Palmyra, New York, Lucy started a "cake and beer shop," where her family sold vinegar sour pickled eggs, sweet breads, and other typical tavern foods. This portable "tavern stand" could be moved from area to area depending on the public event in the village.[25] When Lucy later lived in Missouri, she considered her "business" that of "keeping tavern."[26] She was not raised in an agricultural family, and when she moved onto the farm with Joseph, it would be natural for her to push for including her own experience in their economic efforts.

Like Lucy, Joseph's ancestors were also not farmers by profession. Like her father, three generations of Smith men in America had built bridges, houses, and other structures of heavy timber construction. Asael's father arranged for his apprenticeship to a good cooper refining the family woodworking skills into detail-oriented piecing work, and Asael learned to make barrels, a craft he taught his sons. The probate records at the deaths of the Smith men document plenty of woodworking tools, but few farming implements.[27] And the agricultural tools they left behind were largely associated with raising cattle—an activity they did on the side instead of as their primary industry.[28] Joseph and Lucy also only had about five acres of easily tilled flatland, and this was wetland that would not sustain crops, the rest was rocky hillside with no evidence of tillage.

When Lucy said they began to cultivate the soil, she clearly did not mean fields of wheat for the grain market. She and Joseph planted a perennial crop that needed weeding and tending but not constant soil preparation. We don't know what Joseph and Lucy decided to grow for that brief period. But when we consider the family background, the physical evidence of their land, and what we know of the earliest cash crops grown in the Tunbridge mountains, they probably grew cider apples or hops.

The Smiths had an apple orchard. They could have had one in the meadow where apples are growing wild today. But they could have also planted apples on the hillsides of their property. The rough nature of the hills' surface is consistent with what would be seen if a pasture had been turned into an orchard. In East Randolph, three miles west of the Smith Tunbridge farm, merchants on the turnpike purchased cider from Richard Lang, a wholesaler in nearby Hanover who did business with storekeeper Jesse Smith, Joseph's oldest brother.[29] Lang could have acquired some of his cider from the Smith family that he sold to other merchants. Since Joseph quit tilling the land after six years to operate a store on the turnpike, perhaps he moved from cider production to cider marketing—or tried to travel back and forth the three miles during harvest to do both.

The other possibility is Joseph and Lucy raised hops on their hillsides. While the evidence of hop farming is also circumstantial and inconclusive, there are intriguing possibilities. Hops were the first cash crop grown in Tunbridge.[30] Hop rhizomes were imported from Massachusetts about the time Joseph and Lucy Smith began to till the soil, and they were grown in several towns in the county. Massive, ancient hop rhizomes are still occasionally discovered in the Tunbridge woods marking now lost locations of what were called "hop grounds" in 1800 and are known as hopyards today.[31] A hopyard needs to be well drained, and while they're usually established now in large, flat fields where modern equipment can freely operate, in 1800 a hillside would have been an ideal place for a yard.[32] Since water flowed off the Smith hillside into the fen below, it was naturally a well-drained area and would have required less effort to prepare than a large flat field.[33] Most early hop growers also worked closely with a dairy because hops needed lots of manure to grow well, and dairies produced an overabundance of the resource.[34] Hop bines grow vertically as 20–30-foot-tall vines supported by poles, and a cooper with a draw knife and a shave horse could prepare hundreds of poles quickly. He would need more than a thousand per acre. But Joseph had everything he needed to build a large hopyard quickly.

Joseph also had all the necessary requirements to produce his own beer if he chose. He had a cool, productive spring and access to plenty of barrels. Hannah Glass's cookbook used widely when the Smiths lived in Vermont instructed brewers to use hogsheads and barrels at several stages of the beer brewing process. A cooper could readily make his own brewing equipment as well as the kegs needed to ship the final product. Glass's recipes used hops, sugar, and water as the main ingredients for her "small beers." Other cookbooks outlined recipes for "root beer" that use ginger as their base but include yeast made from hops.[35] This beer was a popular fare along with gingerbread at local militia gatherings in the spring and religious camp meetings throughout the year.[36] It was also the beer Lucy made and sold at her tavern stand in Palmyra.[37] Her beer in Palmyra "commanded brisk sales," as evidence of her skill in production.[38]

Beer was also drunk freely by travelers. The settlement in East Randolph where Joseph and Lucy Smith moved after they abandoned their agricultural pursuits was on the "old turnpike" from Burlington to Hanover that was a "place of considerable importance" to travelers going through Vermont. It was only three miles from their farm, and they could work back and forth as needed. There was another distillery further up the street, and seven additional businesses in the village that sold alcohol to travelers. These businesses primarily sold whiskey (including varieties they called potato whiskey, rye whiskey, and corn whiskey), and a beer brewer would have a ready market of what was considered wholesome family drink in a high traffic village on the eastern edge of Randolph Township.[39] Vermont embraced prohibition early and long which limited the information preserved on these early establishments and their products. But the limited information from this early period suggests the Smith store on the turnpike likely sold drink to travelers and brewing may have been part of their activities as it was later in Palmyra.

Demand for hops outpaced supply about the time Joseph and Lucy began to work their land. William Goodwin advertised in the *Green Mountain Patriot* on June 14, 1800 for "3 tons of good well dried HOPS, by the first of January [1801]."[40] Joseph would have initially had a ready demand for his crop which may have encouraged his efforts to grow the vines. In 1798 dried hops were selling for from 12-14 cents a pound, a high price for an agricultural product when one of the only ones to sell for more was ginseng which sold at 18-33 cents a pound.[41] By September 30, 1802, prices for hops had dropped to six cents a pound as competition increased significantly. Prices did not recover for another decade after many growers stopped production.[42] Joseph and Lucy rented their farm and started their store on the turnpike in East Randolph right when the price of hops experienced a temporary downturn, suggestive of a possible relationship between the two events.

The rough nature of the Smith hillsides is as consistent with hop production as it is with apple growing. Hop bines are a perennial crop, and in Joseph and Lucy's day they were farmed by weeding around the plants with a hoe, but the soil was not plowed each year. They could be brought into production quickly. And with a rapid drop in market value at the time the Smiths moved to Randolph, they could have been abandoned quickly as well. Other hop farmers in the nineteenth century abandoned their hopyards as prices fell.[43] There is evidence that an oast (a building used to dry hops) operated on the Smith farm, as is discussed in Chapter Six: A Smith Industrial Building. A pollen study and additional research on the Smith property may yield a definitive possibility.[44]

Chapter Four
The Smith Log Cabin

Historical Evidence

Lucy praised her husband's handsome farm where they started out as newlyweds, but she said nothing of the house her husband provided for her where she would have primary responsibility. Joseph's younger brother John remembered its appearance when the family arrived unplanned in late October or early November 1791 and found a "little cabin that my Brothers had built for their own accommodation while to work on the land." It was not built to get a large family through a long Vermont winter. It was "l[o]osly built after the mode of building log huts say 14 feet by 10[.] the covering was the bark of the elm."[1]

Ten-year-old John's first view of his family's new home recalls that of Elias Smith (not a relative), a neighbor three years older than John. Elias lived in nearby Woodstock township, and had an older brother who also accompanied a father from Massachusetts to buy land in Vermont. Elias's brother also built a cabin for his family while his father returned home to bring the family to Vermont. Elias recalled: "After many sweats and hard pulls, my father pointed us to the house, about forty rods ahead, the sight of which struck a damp on my spirits, as it appeared to me only an abode of wretchedness. After going to it and taking a general view of the house and land around . . . Though I was some over thirteen years, I cried."[2]

Elias's brother knew his family was coming that year and built a permanent log home with squared logs and locked corners. His family's house was better built than the temporary hut John first saw. John may never have seen a log structure before. Americans adopted log construction after Asael and Mary's ancestors had already built permanent homes in New England.³ The Tunbridge homes were probably the first log buildings many of the local settlers had seen, and the Smith hut was certainly the first one Joseph and Jesse Smith built. Their neighbors went through the same learning process when building their own homes. One early Tunbridge settler spent his first winter living in a sap tub until he learned how to build a log home. Royalton historian Hope Nash concluded this unnamed settler and other early hill settlers learned to make their cabins from French Canadians.⁴ The Smith boys likely used their neighbors' elm bark roofed cabins as models.⁵

Bark Roof Log House
Orsamus Turner, Pioneer History of the Holland Purchase
(Buffalo, NY Jewett, Thomas and Co., 1850), 564.

Several Tunbridge settlers called their first residence a "log hut" or a "shanty."⁶ Others remembered these buildings as a "log cage" or expressed efforts to "fix up the cage."⁷ These structures all seemed more like outbuildings than homes—more like an animal cage or the township pound than a place for people.⁸ They generally had thin doors of bark sheets or rawhide. Some lacked brick hearths or even a fireplace; most lacked windows; they all lacked plastered walls, paint, and the more refined elements of a log house.

When a neighbor of the Smiths, Elijah Tracy, first brought his wife to Tunbridge to introduce her to their "log hut," according to his descendants they walked through the forest for a long time until "the young wife inquired, 'How long before we shall come to the road?' 'Why,' replied the husband [Tracy], we have been in the road all the time.' With unfaltering steps she pursued the course until they arrived at the spot on which stood the rude hut of logs." Unable to remove a log stump at the site, Tracy left it in the center of their hut to serve as their table.[9]

A log cabin was more functional than a hut. It may have had a dirt floor or sometimes puncheon (half logs smoothed with an ax or adze) and few windows or other ways to let light into the structure. But it was a nicer setting with more refined furnishings. No single characteristic made a building a cabin rather than a hut. It was usually a matter of degree and feel. A log cabin also appeared rustic and primitive when compared to a log house. It was still the kind of place that might make a boy cry when he saw it.

The elm bark Joseph and Jesse Smith used on their hut was typical roofing for Iroquois longhouses, and the style was widely used by the first settlers of Vermont. These settlers cut the elm bark into large sheets and laid it flat over rafters with the smooth side down and fastened at regular intervals with long poles over the whole. Such roofs were watertight and could be built without using nails.[10]

Eleven members of the Smith family arrived just before the Vermont winter of 1791. (Priscilla Smith stayed behind in Ipswich, Massachusetts, to take care of her sick aunt, Priscilla Kimball.)[11] Jesse was already courting Hannah Peabody of Middleton when he accompanied his father north to buy land, and he returned to Massachusetts that winter to marry her on January 20, 1792.[12] Hannah's father Benjamin Peabody was a cooper who specialized in placing iron hoops on barrels. He lived a few miles from Topsfield and the Smiths may have taken their barrels to him to finish when they needed iron hoops rather than the standard hazel or ash withies that wrapped most barrels.[13] It is likely Jesse met Hannah through her father. Jesse and Hannah returned to Vermont in the spring to settle on lot 19 just east of the original lot.

But even after Jesse left for the coldest months, ten people lived in 140 square feet of space that first winter. Archaeology suggests the family initially slept around an open fire with smoke going out of a hole in the roof with barely enough room for everyone to lay on the dirt floor at the same time. The family had an urgent need to expand and refine their living space. Besides space for a large family, they needed a suitable hearth and fireplace to cook food (most cooking was done on the hearth not over the fire), they needed a cellar to preserve food before the next winter, and they needed workspace to produce textiles, tools, and other objects of daily living. At some point very early in their occupation of the site, the Smith family expanded their house to address an urgent need for space. This probably happened during the summer of 1792.

Other Smith Homes

One reason the Smith family moved to Vermont was to get their sons land to marry and establish households.[14] Asael soon began buying additional property. On November 29, 1794, he purchased lot 17 North just west of the initial Smith farm and only paid twelve pounds for it— less than half of what he paid for his first lot.[15] The property was a single mountain with no flat areas, meadows, or springs. Then on December 17, 1795, he made his most significant purchase. Asael bought lot 10 in Tunbridge, which was one-hundred acres just above lots 17 and 18 North.[16] The lot was mostly low undulating hills with large flat areas in the center. Less than a month later, and ten days before Joseph and Lucy would marry, Asael wrote a letter on January 14, 1796, to a distant cousin Jacob Towne, Jr., in Topsfield, Massachusetts, informing him, "my Son Joseph will Live on the old farm (if that that hes bean but 4 years. occupied Can be Called old)."[17] Joseph would pay for it on "halves," Asael wrote, meaning Asael and Mary cover half the cost to help their son get started, and Joseph would pay for the other half himself as was then customary.[18] So, when Lucy said her husband "owned a handsome farm," he had possession of it but was still buying it and did not yet hold title to the land which was kept in Asael's name.

Asael probably wrote his letter to Towne so his son Jesse could carry it, since the day after Asael wrote the letter Jesse was in Middleton a few miles from Towne taking out a mortgage on his property (lot 19) from his father-in-law, Benjamin Peabody.[19] This was the beginning of extensive and ultimately tragic changes to Smith Settlement.

Joseph Smith and Lucy Mack married on January 24, 1796.[20] Asael suggested in his letter to Jacob Towne that the couple "will" live in the old home. He had only purchased lot 10 a few weeks before the marriage. So, it is likely Joseph and Lucy shared their first home with the larger Smith family for a time while Asael and Mary built a new home on lot 10. Two years after Joseph and Lucy's marriage, Elijah Tracy surveyed a public road for the township that ran through the Smith property, probably simply repairing the road that had developed naturally during the initial land clearing period. He began his survey on March 13, 1798, at the northeast corner of what he called the Asael Smith house, since the deed was in Asael's name, although Joseph, Lucy, and their one-month old baby Alvin were likely all that were living there by then.

Tracy surveyed from the northeast corner of the house, along its east side running south, down through Joseph and Lucy Smith's lower meadow; then turning east as the road rounded the hill, he followed it northward to where it connected to the main road between Tunbridge village and South Tunbridge which were known early as respectively The Market and Jigger village.[21] Early roads became slicks of animal manure compacted with hooves and heavy wagons, so that two centuries later subtle differences in foliage are still visible in aerial photographs. Laying Tracy's survey coordinates over aerial photographs highlights the original road still visible in the plant growth along the route. Using Tracy's coordinates puts the northeast corner of the Smith home at 43°52'18.65"N latitude and 72°32'18.03"W longitude.

The foundations of the home Tracy marked in 1798 were photographed by George Albert Smith and German E. Ellsworth in June 1907.[22] Their photograph preserved significant details about the home that were lost during the 1960s when the township widened and paved Ward Hill Road in front of the house and rerouted parts of the road out of wet, muddy areas.[23] The widened road partially covered the southeastern edge of the foundation. And during road construction heavy equipment pushed part of the foundation into the cellar and covered it with backfill pushed in from around the homesite.

Archaeological Evidence

In late October 2016 we visited the original Smith property and looked at the surface evidence carefully. We found the stone foundation in similar condition to when it was photographed in 1972 by historian Larry Dahl.[24] Because the landscape is still riddled with the remains of the homes of many of the first settlers—sometimes found as entire communities deep in the woodlands—we confirmed the foundations were on the Smith property, and a preliminary test trench uncovered part of what would prove to be the north cellar wall. We found several fragments of early ceramics suggesting it was likely the site where the Smith family settled.[25] We returned to the foundations the following year and used the Tracy 1798 survey coordinates as a starting point. We laid out a grid of sections five feet square totaling sixty feet long and twenty-five feet wide, and with the assistance of local volunteers we excavated the home foundation and interior cellar during August 6–19, 2017.[26]

Don Enders at Home Site

Archaeology exposed two sections of the Joseph and Lucy Smith home. The smaller section's dimensions were 10 X 14-feet. This section rested on plinth stones about one foot in diameter set at each corner. Its dimensions match those of the original building described by John Smith, and supporting evidence suggests this was the building John mentioned. This section had been remodeled into a kitchen early in its history. The position of the fireplace inside the structure in the center of this section suggests the room would have been too small for the family had they had a chimney inside when they first arrived. The Smiths likely did not have a fireplace during the first winter but used a hole in the ceiling to let out smoke. Since all glass in their valley during the eighteenth century was imported over difficult roads, it is likely the hut originally had no windows.

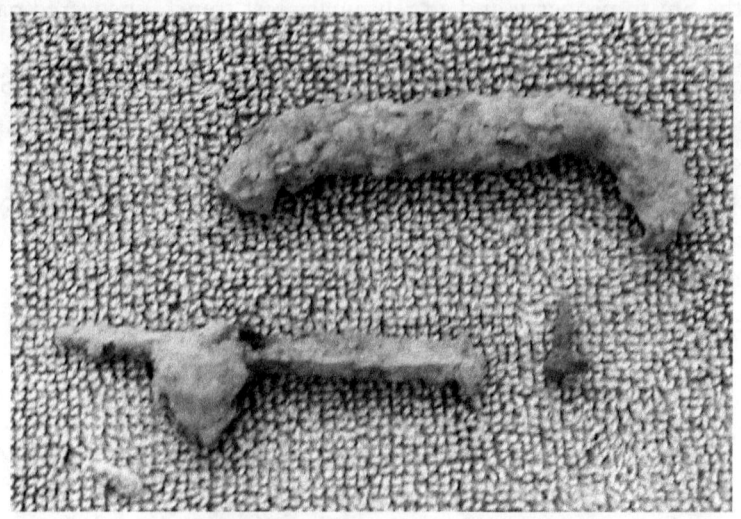

Rosehead Nail, Small Brad, and Iron Handle

We did not find any shingle nails at the site, confirming John's description of a bark roof and suggesting the family did not replace their bark with split shingles later. We found one full-size nail in the backfill—a 2-7/8-inches-long, hand-forged, eighteenth-century rosehead nail. Because it was apparently pushed into the cellar during 1960s road expansion and not found in context, we don't know how it was used. We also found one small brad and an iron handle in the backfill. The brad was possibly used to fasten leather to wood while the handle may have been attached to a chest or trunk.

The Cellar

South of this original home section are the remains of a 14 X 14-foot cellar addition. The Smith family dug a builder's trench thirty-inches deep and stacked massive stones, some weighing more than a ton requiring the help of oxen, a stone boat, levers, and three or four men to place them. The massive stones served as the base for smaller rocks stacked as evenly as possible on top. At the base of the foundation, the builders left an eight-inch lip before digging the center down an additional twenty inches. This gave the foundation more stability, and the lip could have also served as a cheese curing shelf. When the house later burned down, a two-inch layer of charcoal covered the entire site and marked the dirt floor level in the cellar. The 1907 photograph shows the foundation extended above ground about two-and-a-half feet. This required a wood floor and put the floor of the cellar after it was finished approximately eighty inches below the main level, making it easy for an individual six-feet tall to get in and out of the cellar with plenty of room.

Southeast Corner of Cellar Floor Looking East

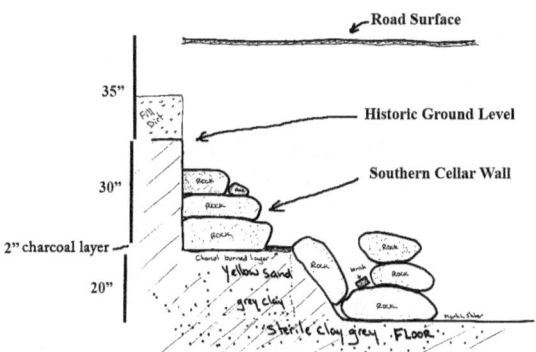

Smith Home Cellar Profile

The Kitchen

The firebox inside the 10 X 14-foot kitchen was made of fieldstones held together with a lime mortar. A brick hearth used as a cooking surface extended in front of it. The Smiths laid one-hundred-and-thirty brick directly on the dirt without mortar to form a hearth 5 X 6 feet. This made an area large enough Mary could cook for a big family with ease. The brick is consistent with late eighteenth-century manufacture.[27] They were made by amateurs. The clay had not been well-worked and still had lumps and particles in it when fired. Surviving brick fragments large enough to study were typically poorly shaped; and with few exceptions they had not been fired at high enough temperatures for long enough to make a good, solid product. Some were likely already beginning to crumble before Joseph and Lucy moved from the site.

Don Enders Excavating the Smith Hearth and Firebox

Smith Family Do-It-Yourself Brick Cross Section

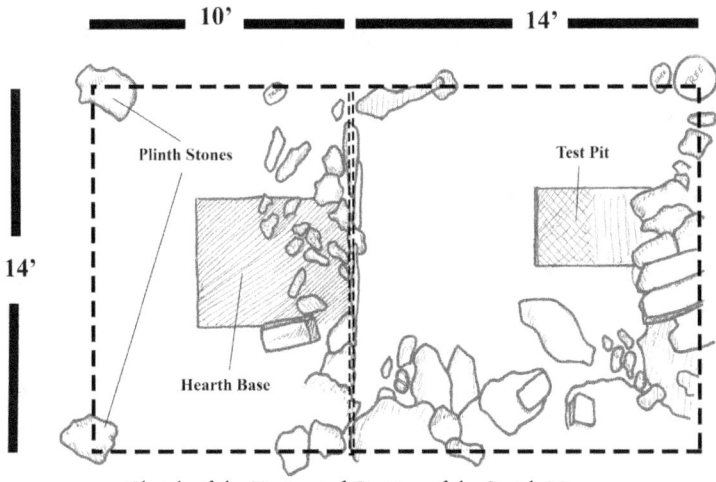

Sketch of the Excavated Portion of the Smith House

New Section of the House

If the home had an upper level, given the lack of nails at the site it was a loft or garret with a floor of puncheon. The east wall of the cellar was covered by roadbed and we could not examine it. Because we didn't find a cellar entrance, however, we assumed it was underneath the road. Evelyn Sargant, who as a child played in the cellar in the 1930s, confirmed this was the case. When we discovered the 1907 photograph while preparing this article for publication, we could see the cellar entrance was indeed in the east wall inside the home close to the front door.

Expanded House Profile, June 1907
Photographed by George Albert Smith and German E. Ellsworth

The photograph also showed a significant portion of the home hidden underneath the widened road we had not seen in the excavation. A long line of foundation stone appears at a higher elevation along the front stoop extending to the south that adds another 10 X 24-foot section to the home. This made the footprint of the Smith home a full 24 X 24-feet with a cellar and possible garret.

Evidence of windows in the home comes from small pieces of hand-blown window glass from two different panes. Their thinness—one measured at 4mm and the other at 6mm thick—and general smoothness are consistent with crown glass. This higher status window glass was made by spinning plates of blown glass into large circles and cutting out small panes. They suggest that at some point the Smiths upgraded features of their home.

When Elijah Tracy surveyed the road through Smith Settlement in the spring of 1798, he wrote he began at the corner of a *house*. He did not note a *cabin*. When Tracy wrote, there was a difference between the two. A log house had more in common with the English architecture of the original settlers than did a log cabin. It had notched logs with squared corners, a wood floor (sometimes puncheon but usually sawn lumber), a wood door, a chimney with a brick hearth, windows, shingles, and painted or plastered interior walls. Tracy saw enough features in the structure to give it a semblance of civility, but the archaeology suggests it barely fit into that category. By the end of its life it still had a lot in common with cabins. It was likely the large size—24 feet square—that suggested a house to Tracy; but windows, an interior cellar access which confirms wood floors, a brick hearth, and other elements may have also contributed to Tracy's perceptions.

Shortly after Joseph and Lucy sold their farm, Vermonters left the Green Mountains in throngs and many homes were abandoned. Their home may have been one of these. There were no artifacts found buried at the homesite dating to a period after they left.[28] At some point the home burned down, leaving approximately two inches of charcoal and ash covering the site buried by more than forty inches of later debris and fill. Farmers often burned structures to clean up a site and protect their animals from getting hurt in the ruins. The fire left the charred remains of a tree stump (at least 30 years old when it burned) growing out of the southern wall of the foundation, suggesting the home had been abandoned for a considerable time before it was lit. A black cherry tree now grows from the foundations next to the charred stump, and is at least seventy-years old, suggesting it started growing shortly after the Ellsworth-Smith photograph was taken in 1907.

Chapter Five
Smith Family Comforts of Life

Lucy Mack was responsible for providing the furnishings in her house. As young women earned money, they often purchased items and stored them in anticipation of furnishing their own "Articles for Housekeeping." The things they brought to the marriage were known as their "bridal portion" or "marriage portion."[1] Although the concept of a dowry had not yet blossomed into what it would become by mid-nineteenth century, it was already moving in that direction and parents sometimes helped with the marriage portion when they could. Lavish furnishings reflected well on a new bride and her parents.

Mary Palmer was born the same year as Lucy but married a little more than a year before her at age nineteen. Mary grew up in comfortable circumstances, and yet her suitor, Royall Tyler, who lived in Woodstock, Vermont, twenty-five miles south of Tunbridge, secretly gave her parents, "a large trunk tightly packed with everything a parent could wish for an outfit for a daughter," so they would look especially generous when they announced Mary's marriage to the community.[2] Even after their marriage, Royall bought Mary a dozen teaspoons and three large spoons all marked with M.P.—her initials before her marriage—so it would look like she had brought them to the household. "This was delicate and kind in him, for he knew I could not purchase them, and he wished to make it appear that my parents did so."[3]

In Lucy and Joseph's case, Joseph's family had helped meet his part of the furnishing by providing half of his house and farm. Lucy's role in providing furnishings included a visit to her parents in Gilsum, New

Hampshire, after Lucy and Joseph married on January 24, 1796. Their trip was not unique. In fact, brief post-marriage trips, especially to visit family, were becoming increasingly common. And the showering of wedding gifts was sometimes done during these visits. It appears Lucy expected such gifts on her visit. When she stopped at her brother and sister-in-law Stephen and Temperance Mack's house, as she and Joseph "were about setting out on this visit," the conversation turned to the "subject of giving [Lucy] a marriage present."[4]

Mack's business partner John Mudget offered to give Lucy a gift of $500, and Stephen matched the amount. They more than filled her parents' role with a check for $1,000 that brought as much public honor to the family as that enjoyed by Mary Palmer or anyone else. And yet, Lucy told her readers, after her visit to her parents she didn't need the gift money to set up housekeeping. "I had other means by me," she recalled, "sufficient to purchase my housekeeping furniture."[5] She laid the $1,000 check aside.

Bowl Portion of a ca. 1790 Mack Family Spoon

Lucy may have provided much of her furnishings herself as was expected, but it is possible her parents also assisted. A bowl of a pewter spoon dating to the time of Lucy's marriage was found on the Mack farm in neighboring Sharon, Vermont, where Joseph and Lucy lived for a time after leaving Tunbridge.[6] The gadrooning (the raised decorative pattern) on its back, and the distinctive shape of the bowl, narrows its construction date to the 1780 to 1800 period.[7]

Unfortunately, it is broken right below the stem where initials were usually placed, so we don't see an L.M. on the stem to suggest the spoons were Lucy's (or her mother Lydia's). Because the spoon bowl was removed from its original context by a site visitor, until the rest of the spoon is found we won't know who owned it. But spoons were the most common housekeeping item parents gave to their daughters, and it is possible Lucy's parents followed common practice.[8] Since it was fancy but not silver, it suggests the owners of the spoon lived comfortably but not extravagantly.

Jesse Smith's father-in-law, Benjamin Peabody, cast pewter spoons on the side as one of his many small jobs in addition to coopering. In 1799 and 1802 he made pewter spoons for Brimley Peabody at approximately one shilling each.[9] It is possible he made pewter spoons for Jesse Smith to sell in his store.

When Lucy moved into her new house with Joseph, the garbage already scattered about the ground around their home reflected her mother-in-law Mary Smith's household. But Lucy, Joseph, and their children added to the refuse during roughly five years they lived at the site. It was common to throw garbage out of doors and windows creating a layer of artifacts throughout the yard—the larger work area of the site.[10] One contemporary described the yards of families in the Smith's native Massachusetts as "an inlaid pavement of bones and broken bottles, the relics of departed earthen ware, or the fragments of abandoned domestic utensils."[11] This layer of garbage, known in archaeology as a sheet midden, tells a lot about a family. Patricia and Scott Beavers, who own the property where the Smith home is located, have found ceramic fragments in their garden forty feet away from the homesite. But due to limited time and resources, and to impact the property as little as possible, we only excavated the home site and a six-inch perimeter around the foundation. The artifacts recovered from that area shed light on the Smith family time in Tunbridge.

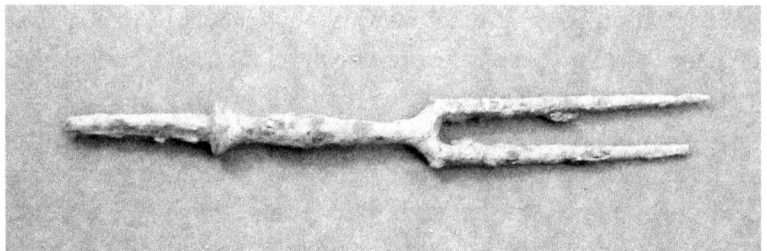

Tines of a Smith Family Fork, ca. 1760s

The earliest datable artifact recovered was a two-pronged fork found in the backfill pushed into the cellar. The "slouched shoulder" design of the fork was the common style from 1687–1710, but the bulbous handle with a long stem was more typical of 1760 or slightly later.[12] Its old style suggests this was possibly something that came with the family from Massachusetts, perhaps a family heirloom dating to Asael and Mary's marriage in February 1767, although it is possible the family acquired it in Vermont. Used furniture and other household items were sometimes sold at moving sales held in local taverns.[13]

The earliest dated ceramics recovered were the remains of two broken bowls found scattered among the stones pushed into the northwest corner of the cellar foundation. They are a type of creamware ceramic called queensware, made during the second half of the eighteenth century. In 1765, shortly after Josiah Wedgewood developed a lighter, white ceramic, he sold Queen Charlotte in England and Catherine the Great in Russia tea sets of this style. Wedgewood then marketed the ceramic to upscale families as queensware. While Chelsea porcelain and "India China" (Chinese export porcelain) were the primary ceramics used by royalty, queensware was used in informal royal contexts and lent it an air of refinement. It also became the ceramic of choice for wealthy and upper middle-class families who used it for social occasions, with a few imported pieces from China worked into the setting to add an extra sense of refinement. Families that used queensware during the early years of production were typically part of the social elite.

Wedgewood continued to make improvements to this creamware, so it changed slightly over time until he developed a final version in 1808 which continued to sell through the first half of the nineteenth century. The pieces found on the Smith property are of the style made between 1770 and 1808.[14] Wedgewood began selling large amounts of this style in America beginning in the 1780s, and it is likely Mary or Lucy purchased the bowls new. The dates more closely match the 1796 to 1802 period of Lucy's occupation of the site.

Queensware Rum Punch Bowl Fragments, 1770–1808

These queensware bowls were "punch bowls." Although many things could in theory be served in this style bowl, they were marketed and most commonly used to serve rum punch at social gatherings. Tunbridge Township paid for rum out of the tax revenue to encourage men to help build the Congregational Church, but they still could not get enough men together to construct it in a timely manner.[15] Most rum was served at private social events. The recipe for rum punch in Jesse Smith's father-in-law's ledger was typical. Benjamin Peabody wrote the recipe down using spelling suggestive of the family's Eastern New England dialect. "Squeeze the Lamons into Something Clean. then Strain it through a fine strainer Nine Ponnds of Shugar to Eleven half Ponnds of juice—a

Quart of Rum to half a Point of juice—"[16] The sugar would have been "white Havana sugar" if available rather than everyday maple sugar.[17] Rum punch always included plenty of water and sometimes a little lemon peel.[18] Asael's friend Jacob Towne paid one shilling two pence for a pint and a half of rum in 1794, about the same price as a bushel of turnips; and a dozen lemons cost about as much as a new barrel.[19] Jesse Smith's distributor of goods for his store was a major shipper of rum and lemons in the region.[20] If the Smiths served rum at social functions, it represented a significant social expense. Such expenses were more likely paid by Asael and Mary, as Asael served as a town selectman beginning April 27, 1793.[21] He continued to fill various political offices during his time in Tunbridge. But social expectations were such that even non-politicians such as Joseph served punch at special occasions. Two days after Lucy delivered her son Harrison (who later went by his first name Samuel), Joseph purchased two quarts of rum for 67 cents—enough for a large party of well-wishers.[22] But the growing financial strain on Joseph and Lucy's family is evident by the time of Harrison's birth in that no lemons were purchased.

Creamware Tea Cup and Saucer Fragments, 1790–1825

Over a hundred small fragments of creamware dishes, some clearly from teacups, were found just outside the kitchen. These creamware ceramics include a blue tinge in the glaze that made them appear whiter. These were typically marketed by Wedgewood as "pearl white" or, when sold by a competitor, as "China glaze." Archaeologists typically call all of these styles pearlware. Pearlware includes blue tones in the glaze that heighten the white hue of the ceramic. Although it was in production from 1775 until 1825, it was one of the most common types of ceramics used from the late 1790s up to 1820.[23] It was rarely undecorated. When the British East India Company stopped importing Chinese porcelain in 1791 because of high tariffs and the beginning of an American China trade, pearlware was painted in Chinese styles or in other colorful patterns and sold as a replacement. The all-white Smith teacup examples were possibly eighteenth-century acquisitions.[24] Fragments not clearly from teacups may have been plates, saucers, or other eighteenth-century items, but because chamber pots were left undecorated well into the nineteenth-century, some of the fragments may have been night ware.[25] The teacups could have been used by either Mary or Lucy for social gatherings with women from the neighborhood or larger community and would have been ideal companions to the punch bowls for the men.

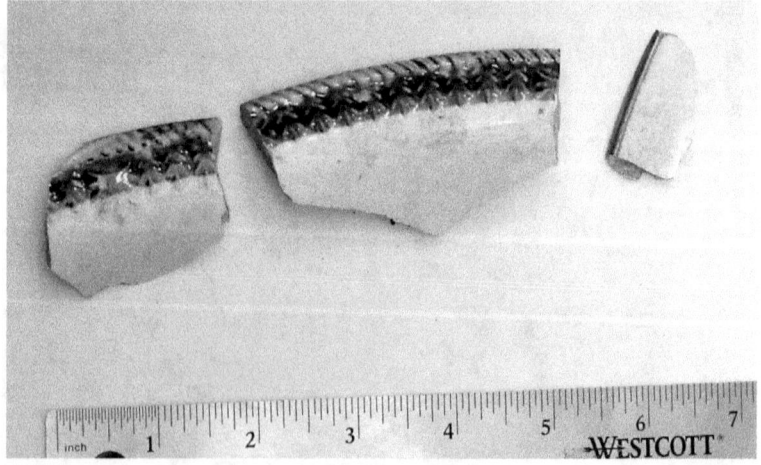

Edgeware Serving Platter Fragments, 1780–1810

In the disturbed backfill pushed into the cellar were three shards of an edgeware dish. The largest of these fragments was three inches long. The curvature on the pieces indicate they came from a serving platter used for social functions rather than smaller dinner plates. Their glaze has blue tones that add a pearl-like luminescence marking them as pearlware. On the rim and extending to the marly (the slanted section between the edge and the well or bottom where food is placed) is a cobalt strip that was the most popular feature of edgeware in the late eighteenth and early nineteenth centuries. Its embossed rim design was first introduced in the 1780s but was quickly replaced by the more popular feather and shell edge designs.[26] The fragments most likely date to the 1790s.[27] Mary could have purchased the platter shortly after arriving in Vermont, or Lucy could have acquired it just after her wedding.

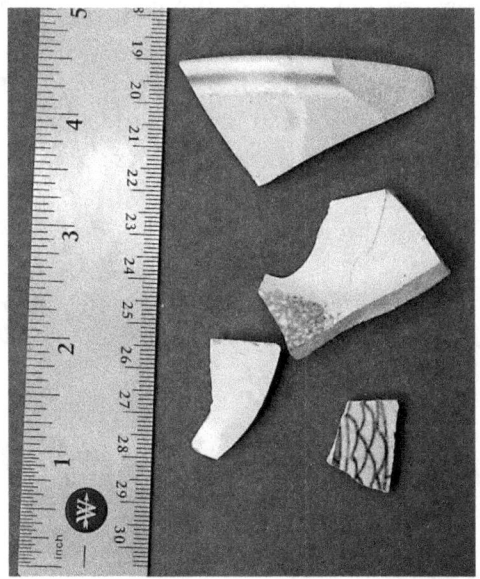

Banded Ware and Hand Painted "Blueware," 1760–1830

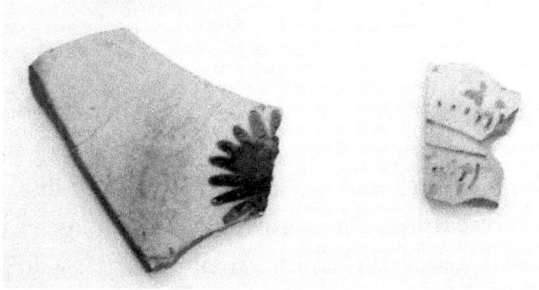

Local Hand Painted Vessels, undated

Six decorated shards were found among the remains of the fireplace hearth. One of these was a bandedware fragment; three were slipware fragments (these had been burned in a fire); and the remaining two were pearlware pieces with hand-painted decoration. It is difficult to date these pieces with any precision. The bandedware is in a style popular as early as the 1760s and uses colors popular during that period, but bandedware continued in production well into the nineteenth century. The pearlware pieces with hand painted cobalt decorations underneath the glaze are reflective of a trend of "blue painters" becoming active in the Staffordshire, England, potteries beginning in the 1770s. These hand painted pieces became much less common after 1812, as print patterns found in transferwares flooded the market. But hand painted pieces were still made into the 1820s.[28] The shards of ceramic with hand painted brown decoration are not English imports and seem to be locally made ceramics, but it is not known where or when they were made.

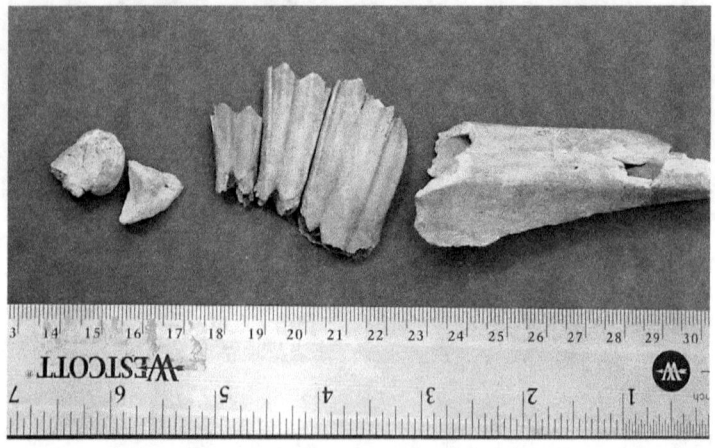

White Tailed Deer Bones, undated

The only food fragments recovered were remains from three white tailed deer (*odocoileus virginianus*), the proximal shaft of the left tibia of one, the teeth of another, and the distal phalanx and distal portion of a medial phalanx of a third. The teeth are from a young animal about one to one-and-a half-years old.[29] These remains suggest wild game was important in the Smith family diet.

Chapter Six
A Smith Industrial Building

Joseph and Lucy Smith had a large building south of their home near their southern boundary. Only the foundations survive today. We uncovered the surface of the three accessible sides of the foundation and dug three test trenches to learn its general features. The first trench was along the northwestern wall where we dug a twenty-feet long, one-foot wide, and two-feet deep trench following the base of the foundation along the inside of the building. The second trench was through the center of the building where we dug a twenty-feet long, one-foot wide, and eight-inches deep trench down to undisturbed soil. This trench straddled the southeastern foundation wall, with ten feet of trench inside the foundation and ten feet outside. The third trench followed along the inside of the southern wall where we dug it two-feet wide by five-feet long and three-feet deep to the base of the foundation at the southwest corner.

This preliminary study shows the building's north wall is 253 feet southeast of the Smith home. Because it goes underneath the current roadbed, we couldn't follow it to its end, but 21-feet-8-inches of the wall is still exposed. Given the location of the building in alignment with the historic road and with the log house to the northwest, it was likely 24-feet long. The south wall is 20 feet further south and 94 feet from the southeastern property line.[1] The 24 X 20-feet dimension suggests the gable end of the building faced the road, a typical orientation for industrial buildings of the period. A preliminary investigation suggests this building could have been an early cider house, an early oast, or an early ginseng drying facility—or all three.

The building had a substantial foundation approximately two-feet wide and two-feet deep. It was made of massive stones, some weighing more than a ton, each laid end to end. The ground was leveled in the area with ground limestone before a builder's trench was dug and the foundation laid. The foundation's substantial size is consistent with an industrial building of the period.

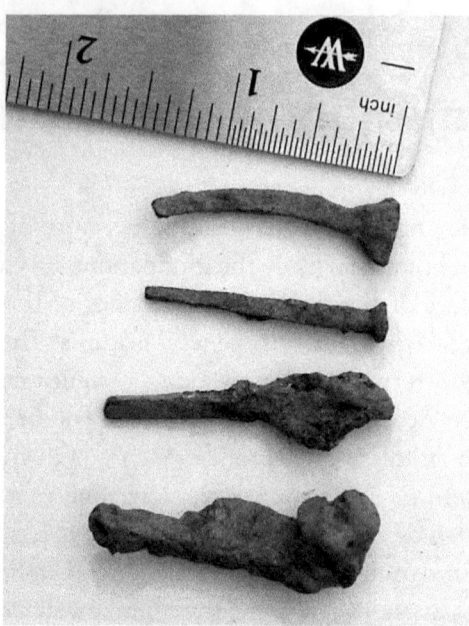

Handworked Cut Nails, 1790–1830

The building had a dirt floor. We found a small fragment of pearlware and four nails that had fallen into the dirt and were pushed up against the southern foundation wall during work in or sweeping of the building. The nails were all approximately one-and-a-half-inches long and were cut nails, suggesting they were made after new nail technology was introduced in the area around the beginning of the nineteenth century.[2] Two of them were clouts, small nails used to fasten thinner boards such as shingles, clapboard, and shipping crates. They could also be used to hold a barrel head in place. The third nail was used for animal shoes, either for oxen or horses. And the fourth nail had a turned head in an L-shaped style often used as a flooring cleat. But had there been flooring there would have been a lot of L-nails in the area not just one. The style was also used for doors and other areas where wood experienced movement to keep the nail head from working through the wood. Coopers used these L-shaped nails to hold hoops in place when they loosened on a barrel. The nail suggests a barrel may have been in the building. But barrels were part of the work of each of the potential uses of the site. They would also be found in a building that had been reworked from one use to another.[3] They do not help narrow the possibilities.

The primary clues to the building's use are its massive foundation and dirt floor. Artifacts found in the dirt and a lack of flooring nails suggest there were no floor boards in the building. If the staves for a barrel were set in the dirt before it was assembled, their smooth edges would be damaged, or grit would get in the way of creating a tight fit. It would be hard to get a barrel that could hold liquid in that setting. A dirt floor eliminates the building as a potential cooperage and suggests if a barrel was in the building it was more likely a finished item than one in production. A dirt floor was also not typical of a barn. Barns of that period were small structures used to hold feed and grain. They had a winnowing floor where the grain was separated from the chaff. A dirt floor would make it impossible to keep the grain clean. The barn was usually built with a floor resting on a plinth stone at each corner and did not need the massive sized stones in this full foundation. Animals were not kept in a barn but in a stable which had a dirt floor with loosely constructed walls and a partial roof to protect the animals from the worst weather.[4] Stables did not have foundations and the floor would not be leveled as manure was regularly removed from them.

In addition to the dirt floor, the heavy stone foundation suggests an industrial building with a second floor. The foundation of the northwest wall had limestone ground down onto the large stones to help level their surface, so they could hold something heavy. The leveling substance continues for several feet out onto the floor as though a mortar had been poured on the ground in that area. We did not excavate further into the building, but this kind of extra effort to create a level foundation is not typical of either a barn or a cooperage. It would be found, however, where a large press or kiln operated and needed to be level.

A cider press needed to operate on a level surface, so the apple cider would flow in the right direction. It would also have a dirt floor to absorb spilt liquid and the family would bring finished barrels into the structure to fill with pressed juice. But a cider press did not need a second floor. A kiln also needed a level surface to keep it stable as it changed temperatures quickly and held heavy amounts of wood or charcoal. Both an oast and a ginseng drying facility used kilns. The kiln in an oast was usually placed against an interior wall with stovepipes running beneath the floor of the second level, so heat could rise through slats of the floor up to where the hops dried. A second floor was an essential feature of an oast.[5] Although less is known about how ginseng drying took place, if it was not done properly the entire batch could be ruined.[6] It usually took several days to dry each batch of ginseng, and Lucy later recalled how her husband had crystalized a large quantity of ginseng which would have required access to a kiln and building much like the setting found near their homesite.[7] Additional archaeology may eliminate some of these possibilities or add more.

Chapter Seven
Selling Smith Settlement

Asael and Mary Smith Building Complex
George Edward Anderson, 1908
Courtesy LDS Church History Library

The history of Smith Settlement gives additional clues as to how Joseph and Lucy Smith used their farmland and the buildings on it. Asael and Mary Smith expanded their holdings when they purchased lot 10 in Tunbridge shortly before Joseph and Lucy's marriage. After the marriage, Asael and Mary finished building their house, added a cooper shop, constructed outbuildings, and refined their work yard which became the anchor of their holdings. George Edward Anderson photographed the Smith complex on lot 10 in 1908 during all seasons of the year. He mistakenly captioned most of his pictures, "Hyrum Smith Birthplace, Tunbridge Gore."¹ This has prevented a proper identification of the site for more than a century. But a comparison of the photograph with the landscape, existing fence lines, and surviving buildings, confirms Anderson photographed Asael and Mary Smith's property on the southern Tunbridge line and not Joseph and Lucy Smith's property in the gore.

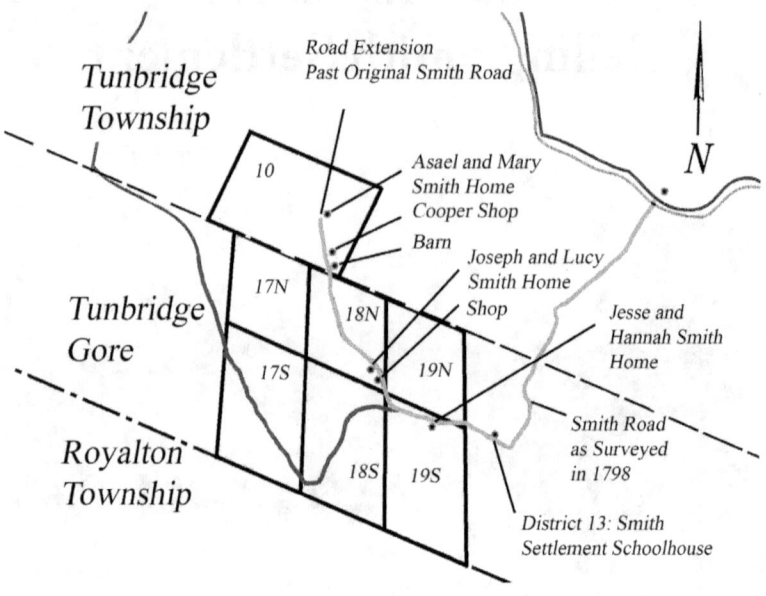

Smith Settlement, 1801

Anderson's photographs capture the building complex on lot 10 in Tunbridge Township much as it looked a hundred years earlier. The barns, a milkhouse, and a cooperage were all in the south end of the complex with the home toward the north off by itself.² The Asael and Mary Smith complex was the heart of Smith Settlement and it played a role in the final disposition of the settlement which had its beginning on January 15, 1796, nine days before Joseph and Lucy's wedding, as Asael and Mary were still preparing to move onto their property. Jesse took out a mortgage on lot 19 North that day from his father-in-law, Benjamin Peabody. This mortgage and a series of subsequent mortgages were arranged by the landowner selling property to an investor at a significantly reduced rate. The seller agreed to pay interest and redeem the property at a given point. If the agreed amount wasn't paid in full, the lender then owned the property.

Over time, Jesse Smith's father-in-law Benjamin Peabody became the primary investor in the Smith Settlement properties. Peabody described himself in the records as a "gentleman." He listed several of his business partners from his village in Middleton and in neighboring Topsfield as "yeomen." This emphasized Benjamin's self perception of a higher economic status and as the principle investor.[3] Benjamin Peabody's business ledger from the period confirms that he continued to live and work in Middleton. He may have never visited his Tunbridge investment properties. The ledger and various property deeds in Vermont and Massachusetts document his business activities with individuals in Middleton, Topsfield, and Salem. And they outline his support for his younger brother Joseph Peabody, who had moved to neighboring Salem where he would eventually become the richest shipping magnate in the world.[4]

Peabody loaned Jesse forty-five pounds on January 15, 1796, with land as collateral, and Jesse promised to pay his father-in-law back in $150 Spanish milled dollars. The specific requirement that Jesse repay in Spanish silver recalls the Peabody family's pepper trade in Sumatra and tea trade in China, where Spanish silver was the preferred medium of exchange.[5] Almost three years later, on December 29, 1798, Jesse went back to his father-in-law to mortgage the rest of his land—one-hundred acres in lot 19 South.[6] The records of this mortgage don't survive. But its later settlement suggests Jesse got an additional $200 in loans for the hundred-acre portion.

It appears Jesse got the loans to open a small general store. If he purchased all his goods for the store from the $350 he got from Benjamin Peabody, it was a small operation but offered a diverse selection. Although the early records of Jesse's store don't survive, he carried some of the outstanding accounts over into an 1807 ledger which lists pepper, cloves, ginger, and tea among the items he sold—things he could get from his Peabody in-laws in Salem. But Jesse also sold shoes and vests, brandy and rum, potatoes and pork, barrels of all sizes, and a variety of foods and goods common to a general store of the period.[7]

A few months after Jesse mortgaged his property to his father-in-law, he took out a second mortgage on the same property from Richard Lang, a merchant in Hanover, New Hampshire. Lang had one of the finest homes in Hanover and a large two-story general store that eventually became part of Dartmouth College.[8] Lang was born in Salem, Massachusetts, where his brother Daniel still operated a store. They used two wagons to bring goods up to Hanover on the rough roads on a regular basis, and Richard sold goods to other merchants in the region.[9]

Jesse Smith had a long relationship with Richard Lang and probably took out the second mortgage to expand his store. Lang provided merchandise and the oldest Smith boy owed him money as is evidenced by a brief letter in Lang's papers.

> My Worthy Friend Mr Lang Sir I have Bin to Canada and have had Verey Bad Luck for I have lost one good horse that wase worth fifty Dollars and cant sell my cow seed as I Expected But I have got a quantity of furs wich I expect to sell and as soon as I can get through with my Busnes I shall come home and mean to settel with you from your frind and well wisher Jesse Smith

March the 23d 1797

Jesse mailed the letter on March 25, 1797, addressed: "Jesse Smith from Tunbridge to Richard Lang Hannover Merchant."[10] Jesse evidently was able to settle his debts with Lang after arranging his business, since this note was written almost two years before he turned to Lang to mortgage his property. Jesse had already mortgaged the same property to his father-in-law, but not for its full value, and he apparently mortgaged the rest of the value to cover merchandise from Lang. It is not clear if Lang knew about the first mortgage to Peabody or if Peabody knew about the second mortgage to Lang or not, but Jesse Smith paid Lang the $133.33 back quickly in February 1799.[11] Then on May 11, 1799 Jesse settled both his mortgages with his father-in-law for the entire 183 acres in lot 19 North and lot 19 South for $350.[12]

In November of that year Jesse sold 50 of the 100 acres in lot 19 South to Amos Allin for $200. Allin bought the southern half of lot

19 South on November 27, 1799, and on the same day on the next page of the deed book, Allin sold the property back to Jesse Smith for $200 in promissory notes. Smith gave Allin four separate notes promising to pay $50 in cattle or salts of lye (which could be sold at Stephen Mack's ashery) for each note.[13] This created another mortgage on the southern half of lot 19 South.[14] Three weeks later, recorded on the next page of the deed book, Jesse then took out a new mortgage from his father-in-law for the upper 50 acres of lot 19 South and for all 83 acres of lot 19 North.[15] He got $700 from Peabody and promised to pay it back in full in seven years and to pay yearly interest on the loan. If he failed to make payments, Peabody would keep the land.[16]

Documentation on the buying and selling of the southern half of lot 19 South is sparse, and it's not clear if the $200 owed was ever paid. But within two years of their initial arrangement James Lasell owned all of lot 19 South. On January 31, 1801, Lasell sold the bottom one-third to his brother-in-law Hezekiah Hutchinson for $150.[17] The Chelsea town clerk recorded the transaction in that township's records, and the judge, legal representatives, and witnesses were all from outside of Tunbridge. It is not clear why the transaction was kept quiet in Tunbridge, or what happened to the property during the few years before. In Benjamin Peabody's surviving ledger of that period, he recorded Jesse Smith paid "one year interest" of $42.92 on February 7, 1801.[18] Lasell died on September 24, 1801, but his family continued to live on and operate the farm just east of Joseph and Lucy Smith.[19] On March 11, 1802, Jesse paid "part of the Interest" he owed to his father-in-law, and Peabody entered $16.08 into his accounts.[20] If Jesse was not able to make a full interest payment in 1802, it is unlikely he could assemble the $700 land payment he owed by 1806.

About the same time Lasell died, Joseph and Lucy rented their farm and moved three and a half miles west of Smith Settlement to East Randolph, the largest village in Randolph Township at the time, where they opened a store on the main turnpike from Burlington to Hanover. They lived near John Lasell's sister Laura E. Lasell Moxley and her husband John Moxley, a local Methodist class leader.[21] John Moxley's brother Thomas Moxley eventually bought part of the Smith Settlement living next door to the Lasells. They did extensive business with Jesse Smith as tracked in his merchant's ledger, but it was Joseph and Lucy Smith that were the connection between the Moxleys, Lasells, and Smith family.

On June 1, 1803, Asael mortgaged his property to Massachusetts investors. Thomas Emerson gave Asael $1,000 for lots 10 and 17. Emerson lived in Asael's hometown of Topsfield and moved a large comfortable home onto his Topsfield property that year. He had no apparent interest in ever moving to Vermont. He and Asael may have been childhood friends, or he knew Benjamin Peabody who regularly did business in Topsfield and Salem, because he trusted his loan was secure and his investment sound. Unlike the Jesse Smith mortgage, Asael's was short-term, and he borrowed the money for one year. Asael likely helped his sons Asael Jr. and Silas Smith get property under similar terms as he had arranged with Joseph, since they agreed to pay back $700 of the principle and all the interest by year's end. Asael was to pay the remaining $300 at that time.[22]

Joseph followed his brother Jesse into the merchandizing business.[23] Joseph anticipated a business windfall in the spring of 1804 from his ginseng trade, and Asael or Jesse may have planned on his success to further their own activities or invested in his efforts as well. But Joseph ended up losing everything.[24] The family's carefully balanced web of finances blew apart in the ensuing winds of creditor collections. Within weeks of Joseph getting news of his soured business deal, Jesse sold all 83 acres of lot 19 North and the 50 acres he owned in lot 19 South to William Adams of Hillsborough County, New Hampshire, on March 27, 1804.[25] His deed acknowledged that Benjamin Peabody of Middleton, Massachusetts, still held a $700 mortgage on the property due December 14, 1806. Adams assumed that mortgage and interest to Peabody and after buying the land paid an additional $800 to Peabody.[26]

The next year Joseph and Lucy sold their forty-two acres in the east half of lot 18 North to James Adams for $600. They sold the property under Asael's name on April 29, 1805, not bothering to pay the fees to register the land in Joseph's name, and not registering the transaction until October, suggesting they considered themselves in serious financial straits.[27] When Joseph sold the property, Lucy was several weeks pregnant, and the couple moved to Lucy's parent's farm in nearby Sharon on the Royalton border. Although they did not know Lucy was expecting a son, Lucy may have already known she was with child—adding additional worry to a family in financial trouble.[28]

Meanwhile Jesse moved to buy his father's land by spinning the first thread of a new financial web. He went to Topsfield in Massachusetts and used the $800 he got from William Adams to pay off his father-in-law's mortgage, and he used it to buy the "mortgage deed . . . with a note of hand signed by Asael Smith Asael Smith Jr. & Silas Smith" from land investor Thomas Emerson, as witnessed by Emerson's brother Billey and a Topsfield neighbor Daniel Heath.[29] On September 30, 1805, Jesse then went to Middleton, Massachusetts, and sold his father's one hundred acres in lot 10 and 83 acres in lot 17 to Benjamin Peabody and Asa How for $1,000. It was witnessed by two of Peabody's business partners.[30] The deed was not recorded in Tunbridge until after Jesse completed the purchase by paying his father $500 and transferring the land to Jesse's name on October 11, 1805.[31] Asael recorded selling Joseph Smith's farm to James Adams on the same day, suggesting both transactions were part of the same larger business deal.

After Asael transferred title of his land to Peabody and How, he arranged to secure title of lot 17 to his sons Asael Jr. and Silas. Earlier Silas sold half of lot 17 South to his brother Asael Jr. on July 29, 1803, but the brothers recorded the transaction on December 6, 1805 preparing to sell it.[32] On the same day Asael Sr. sold to Silas the west half of lot 18 North, the land divided with Joseph who had owned the east part.[33] Silas then sold the property to his brother Jesse later that same day.[34] Except for Jesse's original property which he had already sold, and Asael Jr.'s land that he sold the next spring to Moses D. Rowell, Jesse owned all of Smith Settlement properties under his name or that of his father-in-law.[35] Seventeen days later, his sister-in-law Lucy delivered a son on the Mack property in nearby Sharon, Vermont. They named him Joseph after his father.

When Benjamin Peabody purchased lot 10, he apparently arranged for Jesse and Hannah to move into the home on his property. Asael and Mary moved out of what had been their home into the cooper shop where Jesse allowed them to live. He also gave them use of twenty acres of land. According to a brother, Jesse expected when his parents died he would take over the cooper shop and the twenty acres.[36] A few weeks after the major land transactions of December, however, his brother Silas Smith married Ruth Stevens on January 29, 1806. Silas and Ruth moved into the cooper shop, too, squeezing into the workshop with Asael and Mary. Jesse then feared his brother's moving into the cooper shop "would result in Silas getting the 20 acres of land, house and cooper shop which were retained by father, should father die." Although Jesse had agreed to assume his father's outstanding debts as partial payment for the property, Jesse reversed himself and sued his father for the remaining money. Rather than counter sue his own son and "recover back not only the homestead but entire farm," Asael left with Mary and several of his children for Potsdam, New York, where they started over.[37]

Jesse and Hannah Smith's oldest son, Benjamin Peabody Smith, was fourteen and they were expecting their eighth of ten children about the time Jesse's parents and brothers moved away. Another Tunbridge resident had overlooked paying his taxes of one penny per acre on his land. Jesse paid the tax and got his neighbor's land. He sold it back to the unfortunate family at a significant profit, but it didn't seem to solve his financial troubles.[38] Eventually he moved to New York to rejoin his family. Benjamin Peabody then sold the remaining land to other Topsfield investors, and the family divested itself of all its Tunbridge land.[39]

James Adams, who owned Joseph and Lucy's property, lived with his father William Adam's family on lot 19 until Jesse and Hannah moved. James then moved to lot 10. His family purchased lot 10 from the Massachusetts investors and eventually James sold it to his son-in-law Americus K. Howard and his daughter Jane Adams Howard who moved into the Asael and Mary Smith home. He allowed the house on Joseph and Lucy Smith's property to decay as he had no need for it, and it slowly disappeared from the landscape.[40] The land then served as cow pasture for the rest of the nineteenth century.

Chapter Eight
Lucy's Meadow, Her Grove, and Her First Vision

Lucy's Meadow

In New England, a strict division of labor governed many of the daily tasks of wives and husbands when Lucy and Joseph married. While the young couple lived in Tunbridge, the meadow at the center of Smith Settlement was Lucy's space. Historian Laurel Thatcher Ulrich eloquently describes spaces like this.

> "If we were to draw a line around the housewife's domain [in the 17th and 18th centuries], it would extend from the kitchen and its appendages, the cellars, pantries, brewhouses, milkhouses, washhouses, and butteries which appear in various combinations in household inventories, to the exterior of the house, where, even in the city, a mélange of animal and vegetable life flourished among the straw, husks, clutter, and muck. Encircling the pigpen, such a line would surround the garden, the milkyard, the well, the henhouse, and perhaps the orchard itself—though husbands pruned and planted trees and eventually supervised the making of cider, good housewives strung their wash between the trees and in season harvested fruit for pies and conserves."[1]

In Lucy's space—Ulrich's housewife domain—she established her first household, gave birth to her first children, and learned to become a member of the Smith family whose name she now bore. It was here she gained her identity as wife and mother. While Joseph had responsibility for their pastures, their tilled fields, their stone walls, their rail fences, their outbuildings, their sugar grove, their wood lot, their larger livestock, and their means of transportation, Lucy maintained the spaces in their lives closest to hearth and home. When Lucy related to a scribe more than forty years later of her Tunbridge search for spiritual enlightenment, she suggested her meadow played an important role in her prayers and as a symbol in a visionary dream. Understanding the physical nature of her meadow helps us appreciate more fully some of the details of her religious quest.

Lucy's Drive for a "Change of Heart"

Lucy grew up in a family that believed people still had divinely inspired dreams and visions like those described in the Bible. When she was young her older sister Lovisa became so ill the family began preparing for her death. Her sister had visions. Lovisa told her family, "I seemed to be borne away to the world of spirits, where I saw the Savior, as through a veil." During this vision, Jesus spoke and asked the oldest Mack daughter to return and warn others to prepare for death. Lovisa was suddenly, miraculously healed and "continued to speak boldly for the space of three years."[2] Lucy hung onto every word. She recalled more than fifty years later not only the details of her sister's vision, but some of the preaching that followed, and the words of a hymn written by the nonconformist Isaac Watts that Lovisa sang before she died.[3]

A short time later another of Lucy's sisters, Lovina, contracted consumption and began predicting her own approaching death. As her associates gathered around, Lovina encouraged her listeners to experience a "change of heart." Lovina suggested she may have experienced her own change when she was ten years old. Lucy listened intently to her sister as she cared for the frail, emaciated, older Lovina until her last breath. Lucy was thirteen.

Distraught by her sisters' deaths, Lucy was inconsolable. Her older brother Stephen followed up on their mother's earlier charge to care for Lucy and invited her to live with his family for a while in Tunbridge. After returning to her parents briefly, Lucy went back to her brother's family where she may have helped in the Mack tavern serving meals and cleaning tables, in Stephen's textile factory painting fabrics, or at home caring for Stephen and Temperance's children. Temperance already had four children under the age of six and was expecting twins. Since the

Macks named these twins Lovisa and Lovina after the two sisters Lucy so deeply mourned, it is likely Lucy helped with the babies.[4]

While at the Mack home, Lucy "determined to obtain that which I had heard spoken of so much from the pulpit—a change of heart." She listened to the Presbyterian minister Reverend Mr. Jones preach at Elias Curtis's meeting hall in the village center while Tunbridge built a church.[5] When Peter Grow finished the church, Tunbridge hired David H. Williston, a Congregational minister, as its permanent preacher.[6] Presbyterians, Congregationalists, and Universalists shared the building. Asael and Jesse purchased pews in the building to help with construction but did not meet with the mainstream congregations. They would meet with Peter Grow and other Universalists during times made available to them. Lucy did not meet the Smith family in church since she noted her brother "frequently spoke to me of one Mr. Asael Smith an intimate acquantance (sic) of his Whose family I afterwards became acquainted with."[7]

David Williston performed most of the marriages in the township, but Seth Austin, the local justice of the peace, performed one—that of Joseph Smith and Lucy Mack. It is unlikely Lucy expected Joseph to attend church meetings with her. She married before experiencing her "change of heart," and her new husband's religious views did not focus on a spiritual rebirth. Joseph Smith was a Universalist from a family of Universalists.[8] They had joined in Massachusetts and brought their beliefs with them.[9] They were among the first Universalists to arrive in Vermont, and their beliefs began spreading in the Tunbridge area as early as 1792.[10] The first township meetings to address religious diversity were also the ones to address needs in Tunbridge Gore where the Smith family settled. And Asael Smith was elected a town selectman when he helped negotiate a solution that allowed Universalists to acquire pews in the church then under construction.[11] He also helped make lists of Presbyterians and Universalists who would not pay taxes to support the Congregational minister.[12]

Joseph Smith's variety of Christianity had become so successful in Tunbridge and the surrounding area that the Universalist preacher Hosea Ballou began making long circuit rides from his church in Hardwick (later Dana), Massachusetts, to preach in the mountain villages. Soon

Ballou left his congregation to settle about a dozen miles south of Smith Settlement at the north end of Barnard Township where he lived and preached from 1801–1807.[13] Ballou traveled from township to township in the area preaching in neighboring villages as well.[14] Universalists in the "important" village of East Randolph organized on April 1, 1801.[15] This congregation was so successful it continued into the 1880s.[16]

East Randolph was the largest village in Randolph Township at the time and was on the turnpike just northwest of Barnard. It became the center of religious activity in Randolph Township for the first thirty years of settlement where most people living in the scattered villages gathered to worship. When Ballou published his influential book *A Treatise on Atonement* in 1805 and defined Universalist theology for subsequent generations, he went to Sereno Wright in Randolph to print it. Wright was a newly married twenty-six-year-old printer living near the Smith family.[17] Smith Settlement was just up the hollow and Asael and Mary Smith's family probably heard many of Ballou's sermons.

As Ballou traveled from village to village, he met Vermont hero Ethan Allen who had recently published his book *Reason, the Only Oracle of Man*.[18] Allen's book significantly influenced Ballou's thoughts. Ballou also read and greatly admired the writings of Thomas Paine.[19] Both men were deists who believed in a God who created the world but was not involved in people's daily lives. Allen argued nature was "the only true 'revelation' of God."[20] He rejected "all supernatural revelation" and condemned "dreams and visions, which have no other existence but in the imagination."[21] And he argued, only the credulous and superstitious believed these "fictitious images of the mind."[22] Paine also emphasized relying on "the simple voice of nature and of reason."[23] He focused on Enlightenment principles of rational thought when seeking after the things of God. Paine contended Ezekiel and Daniel "pretended dreams and visions" as "a disguised mode of correspondence" in order to speak to the people in Babylon's politically repressive environment.[24] Paine implied these early patriarchs were men of rational thought and didn't really believe in such things as dreams and visions when he encouraged Americans to approach their own politically repressive relationship with England in a rational manner.

Ballou did not go quite as far as Allen or Paine. He accepted that the ancient biblical patriarchs had revelations in the past. But he believed God made humans "reasonable beings." So, they should investigate scripture "on reasonable grounds, and by fair argument" rather than looking to dreams or visions or other modern revelation.[25] Although some of John Murray's Universalists in Massachusetts had dreams or visions in the first years of organization that confirmed their belief in universal salvation, even Murray considered revelation was found in the scriptures, and the Holy Ghost spoke to people through the written word in the scriptures.[26] Ballou distanced himself from all internal religious manifestations other than thought and rational study.[27]

Asael Smith shared Ballou's views. He may have been influenced by Ballou's early preaching in the Green Mountains, or he may have read Ethan Allen's writings on his own and come to the same conclusion independent from Ballou. But when Asael thought he might die in April 1799, he wrote a letter to his family and encouraged them in Ballou fashion to "search the scriptures and consult sound reason." When they did so, Asael assured them, they would "find from scripture and sound reason that Christ had come into the world to save sinners." Reason would lead them to conclude, "he can as well save all as any."[28] Asael insisted through reason his family would come to recognize exactly the principles Ballou espoused—Jesus Christ died for everyone, and so God would save everyone.

Lucy had been a Smith for three years when Asael wrote this letter to his family. She was one of the four in-laws Asael referenced when he wrote to his children "as to Your Marriages," and suggested the four spouses of his children were like them and would follow their partners' inclinations. Lucy and the other three—Jesse's wife, Hannah Peabody Smith, Priscilla's husband, John Curtiss Waller, and Mary's husband, Isaac Pierce—were going to believe as their spouses did, Asael suggested, and "nature will find its own." Asael appears to have assumed Lucy would come around to Joseph's perspective, but Lucy had grown up in a visionary household.

The mountain culture of Lucy's childhood that came from her mother's Gates family, embraced dreams and visions as sources of inspiration and guidance. Jesus Christ had also been pivotal in Lucy's sister's experiences. Ballou on the other hand rejected the divinity of Jesus Christ and adopted a Unitarian perspective that only God the Father was a divine being, distancing his perspective even further from Lucy and her childhood emphasis on Christ.[29] Asael Smith had not asserted Christ's divinity in his letter either, only insisting what Ballou also argued, that he had died for everyone.

Lucy's mountain Christianity was naturally distant from her husband's rationalism when a recently imported religious movement began to find its way into the hills. The same time Ballou arrived to preach Universalism in the area, Barnard also became a regional center for a mountain brand of enthusiastic Methodism. The Shouting Methodists that were making inroads into Vermont had in common with Lucy's relatives an interest in spiritual manifestations that included prayers accompanied by visions or dreams.[30] "Hosea Ballou was still in town and the Universalist church was at its zenith and it was a real achievement which these men [Methodist circuit riders] did to so nearly hold their own."[31]

What became known among local Methodists as the Old Barnard Circuit emanated out of the same community where Ballou kept his house and rode out on his own circle of preaching venues. Methodist circuit riders led sermons in the barn on Thomas Freeman's farm on the northern edge of the township. They also regularly held camp meeting revivals in the maple grove behind George Cox's house on Broad Brook. When not meeting in Barnard their preachers followed a regular circuit of villages delivering sermons, and the Barnard Circuit went up the turnpike through East Randolph. The Methodists held their quarterly conference occasionally in East Randolph while the Smith family lived in the area, and Bishop Asbury preached there on June 19, 1806, when he journeyed through Vermont.[32] Although the earliest quarterly meeting records that survive for the circuit date to 1808, just after Lucy and Joseph left, they suggest there were several Methodist classes that could have drawn the couple's attention—six in Barnard, five in Royalton, two in Sharon, and one in East Randolph.[33] Tunbridge organized a class a few years later, well after Joseph and Lucy had left.[34] The Methodist class in East Randolph disappeared by the late nineteenth century, and its records are now gone, but it was most likely the class Lucy and Joseph attended.

Methodist meetings were often camp meetings held in the woods outside of the primary villages. Beginning in 1800 their camp meetings found success throughout Orange County, particularly in Barnard, Bethel, and moving northwest along the main turnpike. In September 1800 about fifteen hundred people gathered in Vershire, just north of Tunbridge, to hear preaching in the open air.[35] Since the township only had nine hundred- and seventy-two-people in the census that year, including infants and their mothers who would not be camping in the woods, the meeting drew the curious from neighboring towns as well.[36] Those who went from Barnard rode through Tunbridge on their way to the camp meeting.

The Methodists preached a Christianity sharply different from Ballou's Universalism.[37] They emphasized the gifts of the Spirit, getting answers to prayers, and receiving spiritual manifestations. During the meetings north of Tunbridge, "several found Jesus, and others, who had already believed were overwhelmed with his power."[38] When the power fell on them they swooned, fell to the ground, and cried out for mercy or found themselves unable to speak with bound tongues.

Hannah Allen, a resident of Tunbridge who grew up in the Allin house in Smith Settlement, and who attended a later camp meeting to their north with other women who were also "from thee low villedg" [Tunbridge], wrote to her granddaughter "a Bout thee Refamation thear," where she "a tended a fancy meetin" and "had a very Refreashing time in dead [indeed]." Her women friends experienced the spirit and power of Elias. One "cold not keep her seet," others "cold not hould thear Pease they had to rise and speek of the goodness of god." Allen begged in her letter, "Pray for your granmarm Pray for tunbridg that thee good lord mite not leave us so no more."[39]

Hundreds of new converts were added in this way on the Vermont preaching circuits at the opening of the nineteenth century. During these meetings "both the wicked and the wise, fell to the floor" as the power descended on them.[40] A traveler attended "a protracted meeting in Randolph, and heard some good preaching and exhortations, and felt some of the power of God myself; some of the preachers seemed to hold me off."[41]

During the spring of 1801 there was a sharp increase is such mass conversions as the apparent awakening "alarmed" one of the preachers. "I was afraid they had not considered sufficiently what they were doing," he exclaimed. "I rose up and poured in upon them a very warm exhortation and told them we wanted none but such as were determined to save their souls." Eighty-three people still came to the front of the crowd to acknowledge their conversion.[42] Similar excitement seemed to happen in village after village. When a preacher stopped in Bethel in 1802, the township just south of Randolph, he celebrated in a letter the enthusiasm he found everywhere and reminisced how when he was first there in 1799 "religion was in general very languid. We had, indeed, some refreshing seasons, but awakenings were rare." The change started in 1801 when the Bethel Presbyterians organized a camp meeting on Graffy Spring, and they invited the Methodists to join in "and made welcome." During that camp meeting, worshipers were "struck to the ground, and made to cry bitterly for mercy." Others were "laid low by the power of God" and bound in silence.[43]

During these meetings, a knot of men and women writhed in front of a makeshift mourner's bench before the preacher's stand crying for forgiveness and wailing that they might have a change of heart. Between the dramatic sermons with their high screeches and low moans, hymns added to the building excitement. The Congregational parishes of New England still sang in the old style where someone sang out the words of a line in a ponderous, slow rhythm and the congregation repeated it back. The Methodist camp meetings introduced a lively call and response style that included a chorus everyone could quickly learn and repeat in unison.[44] These were often the same hymns written by Isaac Watts that Lucy recalled her sister singing, and she apparently knew them well. Preachers encouraged participants at the meetings to pray for answers and promised they would come directly from God. Their hymns reinforced this. The noise and movement at these meetings was a show that attracted many onlookers, and the commotion could be heard up the hollows to the tops of the mountains. But the preachers also encouraged individuals to go to a grove of trees on their own and pray, promising

God would answer them.⁴⁵ Religious seekers became "accustomed to retire into the woods to pray," and these groves filled with "praying people everywhere."⁴⁶

In the middle of the rising enthusiasm, the vibrant, loud sermons targeted the Universalists. The original publisher of Ethan Allen's book burned the manuscript he still had in his possession and "joined the Methodist Connection." The Randolph Congregational Church minutes for September 8, 1802, use the same language in reference to Universalists that Lucy would later use to describe her husband and his family. Brother Andrew Steel was accused by another member of his congregation of "being a Universalist in sentiment … in favor of universal salvation." He was taken before church leaders which included the Reverend David H. Williston, one of the same preachers Lucy listened to in Tunbridge when trying to get her own change of heart. The Randolph Congregationalists accused Steel of having "forsaken the public and stated worship of god" and having "withdrawn himself from the Christian communion." They concluded he had breached his covenants and violated the principles of the gospel and expelled him from their community.⁴⁷ The sustained attack on the Universalists disrupted their congregation for a year. Their Randolph minister wrote a confession of faith into their minute book and required that every member sign below the confession. While the Universalists were teaching that God the Father and Jesus Christ were two different individuals and the Holy Ghost was the influence of the scriptures, they did not believe in the divinity of Jesus Christ. Each member of the Congregationalists assured by adding a signature in the minute book that he or she was not a Universalist by affirming a list of declarations, including: "We believe that there are three persons in the divine nature the Father the Son & the Holy Ghost who are one god possessing equal presentisms & equally subjects of divine worship adoration & praise."⁴⁸ The plodding, rational Universalists did not worship, adore, or praise with enough enthusiasm.

Within this contentious context, Lucy and Joseph moved to East Randolph early in 1802 and almost immediately began to associate with John Moxley. Lucy's description of him forty years later, as written by her scribe responding to her Eastern New England dialect, was of a "Mr Murksley Methodist exhorter."⁴⁹ He was a tailor who also collected passage at the turnpike toll booth in East Randolph and began leading a Methodist class.⁵⁰ Although there was a Universalist congregation in their village, the couple began attending the Methodist class together. The "natural" inclination of husband and wife to share a religious perspective that Asael expected would bring his children's spouses to his viewpoint, seems to have shifted at that time in Lucy's direction, although she acknowledged Joseph only attended because of her. Joseph joined her "for a few times," Lucy remembered, "in order to oblige me."⁵¹

When Lucy's father-in-law, Asael, and her brother-in-law Jesse learned about this, they "were highly displeased, and said so much concerning the matter." Asael's grandson remembered him as a life-long Universalist, who shortly before his death was still writing "quires of paper on the doctrine of universal salvation." Since sharp attacks against the Universalists were scattered among the camp meeting sermons, it's not surprising that the Smith family took offense. After Asael expressed his thoughts to Joseph and Lucy, he "came to the door one day and threw Tom Pains age of reason into the house and angrily bade him [Joseph] to read that untill he believed it." Asael didn't believe everything in Paine's book himself. Paine challenged the atonement, a doctrine at the foundation of Universalist beliefs and one they considered applied to everyone. But Paine emphasized rational thought and ridiculed religious superstition, a position Lucy may have felt as a direct attack on her experiences in the woods trying to find her change of heart. Joseph decided they should quit attending the meetings. "At this I was considerably hurt," Lucy said, "yet I made no reply."⁵²

"In the midst of this anxiety of mind," Lucy recalled, "I determined to obtain that which I had heard spoken so much of from the pulpit: a change of heart. To accomplish this, I spent much of my time in reading the Bible and praying."⁵³ Lucy developed a deep familiarity with the biblical text that still showed years later when she dictated her narrative history.⁵⁴ Six months after she and Joseph had moved off Tunbridge mountain onto the main turnpike in the valley, Lucy contracted the same consumption that killed her sisters. Shortly afterward, John Moxley knocked on her door "in his usual manner." A feverishly ill Lucy perceived "a dark and lonely chasm between myself and Christ." Peering into the darkness and perhaps expecting but certainly hoping for her sister's experience, she recalled, "as I trained my eyes towards the light (which I knew lay just beyond the Gloomy vale before me) that I could discover a <faint> glimmer," but there was no vision of Jesus Christ. Later that evening she finally heard from Him. A voice spoke: "Seek, and ye shall find; knock, and it shall be opened unto you. Let your heart be comforted; ye believe in God, believe also in me." The voice may have been directed as much at Joseph as it was Lucy. In contrast to the preaching of Ballou, it attested to the divinity of Jesus Christ, but it also treated the Father and Son as two distinct characterizations.

After her experience, Lucy went to visit the wealthy Presbyterian Deacon Experience Davis whom she described as "one noted for his piety." After his death the community raised a monument dedicated to him acknowledging his donation of property to educate the local children. Davis and his wife, Hannah, also left substantial property to an adopted son since they did not have natural children.[55] He was attentive to others and used his wealth to bless the community.

Lucy did not say why she went to Davis instead of the Methodist Moxley. Perhaps it was because Moxley was an unordained class leader and Davis was an ordained deacon.[56] Lucy recalled she was interested in finding someone who would baptize her without requiring she belong to his denomination. Although Methodist deacons could baptize, and Catholic and Anglican deacons could baptize when they were the only ordained person in a community, Presbyterian deacons could not. Lucy may have learned this from Davis. Ultimately, her experience with Davis was disappointing. If she expected him to embrace her visionary experience and its emphasis on the divinity of Jesus Christ, he focused on her well-being but said nothing "in relation to Christ or godliness."[57]

Lucy had heard a voice directing her to believe in Jesus Christ, but Joseph did not seek the same experience. After Joseph shifted his business interests, closed his store, and returned with his family to Tunbridge, Lucy began to focus on his change rather than her own. As she tells the story,

> "I retired to a grove not far distant [from the Tunbridge house], and prayed to the Lord in behalf of my husband: that the true gospel might be presented to him; and, that his heart might be softened, so as to recieve it; or, that he might be more religiously inclined.

"After praying some time in this manner I returned to the house much depressed in spirit; which state of feeling continued until I retired to my bed; soon after which I fell asleep, and had the following dream:

"I thought that I stood in a large and beautiful meadow, which lay a short distance from the house in which we were living; and, that every thing around me wore an aspect of peculiar pleasantness. The first thing that attracted my special attention in this magnificent meadow, was a very pure and clear stream of water which ran through the midst of it; and, as I traced this stream I discovered two trees standing upon its margin, both of which were on the same side of the stream. These trees were very beautiful: they were well proportioned, and towered with majestic beauty to a great hight; their branches which added to their symmetry and glory, commenced near their top and spread themselves in luxurious grandeur around. I gazed upon them with wonder and admiration; and after beholding them a short time, a bright light surrounded one of them, which appeared like a belt of burnished gold, but far more brilliant. Presently a gentle breeze passed by; and the trees encircled with this golden zone, bent gracefully before the wind and waved its beautiful branches in the light air. As the wind increased this tree assumed the most lively and animated appearance, and seemed to express in its motions the utmost joy and happiness. If it had been an intelligent creature, it could not have conveyed by the power of language, the idea of joy and gratitude so perfectly, as it did. And even the stream that rolled beneath it, shared apparently every sensation felt by the tree; for, as the branches danced over the stream, it would swell gently and then recede again with a motion as soft as the breathing of an infant, but as lively as the dancing of a sun beam. The belt also partook of the same influence; and, as it moved in unison with the motion of the stream, and of the tree, it increased continually continued to increase in refulgence and magnitude until it became exceedingly glorious.

"I turned my eyes upon its fellow which stood near opposite; but it was not surrounded with the belt of light as the former; and it stood erect and fixed as a pillar of marble: no matter how strong the wind blew over it, not a leaf was stirred, not a bow was bent; but obstinately stiff it stood scorning alike the zephyr's breath, or the power of the mighty storm."

When Lucy awoke from her dream, "I wondered at what I saw," she remembered. And she pondered its meaning. She believed it was given to her that the trees represented people. The pliable and flexible tree that danced like a Methodist at a camp meeting was her husband who would bend to the "breath of heaven," and the stubborn, unyielding one as stiff as any rational Universalist might be was Jesse. As Lucy remembered it forty years later, Jesse would always resist "the pure and undefiled gospel of the son of God."[58]

Lucy's Change of Heart and Joseph Sr.'s First Vision

When Lucy felt challenged by her husband's family, she dreamed of her meadow—her space—with her husband and his older brother towering at its southern edge. Her space was "magnificent" with its "golden zone" and contrasted with the outside world in which she was threatened by conflict.[59] The western border of Lucy's peaceful meadow included a "very pure and clear stream of water" which still exists today. The brook that flowed from their spring and grew into a rushing stream of water at the bottom of Lucy's meadow still leaves it through a hillock covered by a grove of trees making a bubbling roar. Lucy recalled she went to a grove of "handsome wild cherry trees" to pray. Wild black cherry trees still grow on that hillock just inside the south perimeter of the Smith property, and one grows today up through the foundation of the Smith home. Black cherry leaves are deadly to livestock, and the Smiths would have cleared them from all their pastures to make sure their dairy herd could not access them.[60] But they would have left them in the cemetery. While the Smiths had a woodlot on their property and certainly had a sugar bush where they harvested maple sugar, both were part of Joseph's sphere of responsibility. The cherry trees on the hillock at the south end of Lucy's meadow were not part of their pastures because they had started a cemetery on their property where neighbors from surrounding farms were already buried, and where her firstborn child was buried, an infant that died about five years earlier.[61]

While the succession of hypotheticals that place Lucy in the cemetery just inside her property are not certain, it is not unusual to find a mother at her child's grave, and the suppositions highlight the role death played in the religious searching of her family. Death is a strong theme in Lucy's narrative. Her mother's pending death led Lydia Mack to ask older brother Stephen to care for Lucy at the beginning of the narrative. The pending deaths of Lovina and Lovisa served as powerful revelatory moments that Lucy looked to in her own search. Her own pending death was a pivotal transition in Lucy's quest for redemption. And the place of burial of Lucy's first child seems to have continued as a place of contemplation for her.

Sometime in April 1811, about a month after Lucy delivered her son William, Joseph Sr. had a dream which Lucy described as the "1st vision of Joseph Smith Sen." in her retelling.[62] Lucy had seen Joseph in her dream, dancing and bending to the breath of the Spirit, much like that moving throng of penitents at the mourner's bench in front of the preacher's stand during a camp meeting. Lucy considered Joseph's dreams as God given. He likely did as well.[63] Joseph had embraced Lucy's habit of spiritual dreams.[64] Joseph dreamed his seven living children tasted of the joy of God. But he learned his two children who died as infants would also taste of that same joy.[65] Although he had what could be termed a Methodist dream, Joseph received a Universalist answer. God would save everyone. Lucy's dream in their Tunbridge log home had led her to expect a change of heart in her husband. But the change would happen slowly—after they left their mountain home.

Conclusion

Having a better sense of the house and property where Lucy and Joseph lived while in Tunbridge, Vermont, and understanding that the cemetery on Wade Hill was originally part of Joseph and Lucy's farm at the south end of Lucy's meadow, helps place their religious transformation into its original physical setting. Had they chosen to continue to run the family dairy on their farm and not move three miles west to the small village on the turnpike in East Randolph, the outcome may have been different. They could still have traveled to Methodist or Universalist meetings, but they would not have found themselves in the center of the excitement. While neither of them ultimately joined the Methodists, Lucy was drawn to the enthusiastic expressions of mountain camp meeting culture and incorporated them into her experiences. Joseph also began to have dreams, even if they continued to contain a touch of Universalism. The ruins of their home and the refuse they left behind, help add details to the story of their time in Tunbridge before they began a journey that took them into an unexpected direction.

NOTES

Introduction

1. Junius F. Wells, "The Smith Family in Vermont," in Evelyn M. Wood Lovejoy, History of Royalton Vermont with Family Genealogies, 1769–1911 (Burlington, Vermont: The Royalton Woman's Club, 1911), 645.

2. Ernest Henry, Bedrock Geology of the Randolph Quadrangle, Vermont (Montpelier: Vermont Development Department, 1963), and Mark Staker "Archaeological Fieldnotes, Tunbridge, Vermont, 2016–2017," in author's files.

3. This study specifically focuses on the Joseph and Lucy Smith family that lived in the Tunbridge Gore. Joseph and Hannah Smith, another Smith family not related to Asael and Mary Smith, lived on the north edge of Tunbridge. This Joseph Smith lived up Bicknell Hill Road and is buried in Smith Cemetery on the northern edge of Tunbridge. He died at age 84 on August 9, 1853, and his wife, Hannah, died December 14, 1857. Due to space considerations, we do not deal with the Joseph and Hannah Smith family in the article, but we have been careful to distinguish the records of these two families (see Mark Staker Research Files for extensive information on the Joseph and Hannah Smith family).

4. Stewart H. Holbrook, The Yankee Exodus: An Account of Migration from New England (Seattle: University of Washington Press, 1950), vii.

5. Stewart H. Holbrook, The Yankee Exodus: An Account of Migration from New England (Seattle: University of Washington Press, 1950), 1.

6. The initial study was exploratory to test the site and prepare for a complete excavation. The follow up study was done with extensive help from volunteers. While it snowed during the October excavations, the August research included high temper-

atures and dry conditions that required patience and commitment from everyone who helped.

7. Because the project moved forward quickly, and we were constantly working to maintain careful oversite of every aspect of the work, we did not manage to get the names recorded of everyone who assisted us. But those who helped included the Norris family, the Page family, and the Quayle family. We are grateful for the contributions of all.

8. This study included traversing the property of many neighbors who graciously supported the research while we measured distances as they were recorded in original documents to map out the land as it was originally understood and to recover the path of the original road.

Chapter One: Tunbridge Gore

1. Lovejoy, *History of Royalton*, 44–45. The dollar figures given here are based on the exchange rate between New York Pounds and Spanish Dollars. See the detailed discussion below for more information on state issued money and Smith family land transactions.

2. Ivan Dunklee, *Burning of Royalton, Vermont by Indians* (Boston: George H. Ellis, Company, 1906), 84.

3. Hope Nash places Stevens on property down by the river. But since it is clear the Mohawk worked their way down the river attacking villagers, it is possible Stevens was on another piece of his property, including the mountain meadow he sold to the Smiths. Hope Nash, *The Town of Royalton* (Royalton, Vermont: Royalton Historical Society, 1975), 6–7.

4. Lovejoy, *History of Royalton*, 145–147, 161.

5. Zadock Thompson, *History of Vermont, Natural, Civil and Statistical, in Three Parts, with an Appendix* (Burlington: Stacy & Jameson, 1853), 2:69; see also Hamilton Child, *Gazetteer of Orange County, Vermont, 1762–1888* (Syracuse, NY: The Syracuse Journal Company, 1888), 160; and John C. and Priscilla Waller, No. W.1676, Revolutionary War Pensions, Vermont, pp. 1–46; David Waller, No. S14,793, Revolutionary War Pensions, Vermont, pp. 1–18. David's eighteen-year-old brother John C. Waller, already a Vermont veteran of the war at Rutland and Hubbardton, was downriver at their parents Israel and Anna Buffington Waller's farm. John tried to save his brother but when he could not catch up to the fleeing party, he returned to Royalton to protect the inhabitants from further depredations.

6. Lovejoy, *History of Royalton*, 50, 141–152. Stevens and Marsh both played a role in resolving disputed land on the western boundary between Royalton and Bethel Townships where Stevens represented Royalton interests and Marsh Bethel interests. The dispute was resolved on September 6, 1792, marking the end of the reassessment of most property lines.

7. Lovejoy, *History of Royalton*, 45, 51. Lovejoy only gives his name as S. Gale, but Solomon Gale is the only name in the region on census records that fits (U.S. Census 1790, Stratton, Windham, Vermont).

8. Lovejoy, *History of Royalton*, 46, 51-52.

9. "Elias Stevens to Asael Smith, June 21, 1791, Transfer of Deed," Tunbridge Deed Book, Orange County, Vermont, A:324. Lovejoy, *History of Royalton*, 54. For an example of identical language in an earlier transaction, see Elias Stevens to Peter Whitney, October 22, 1790, Tunbridge Deed Book A:269.

CHAPTER TWO: Asael Smith's First Land Purchase

1. Elias Stevens to Peter Whitney, October 22, 1790, Tunbridge Deed Book A:269.

2. John Curtiss Waller (1762–1836) married Priscilla Smith in Royalton, August 24, 1796; see John C. and Priscilla Waller, No. W.1676, Revolutionary War Pensions, Vermont, pp. 1–46; David Waller, No. S14,793, Revolutionary War Pensions, Vermont, pp. 1–18. See also, Lovejoy, *History of Royalton*, 130–147, 161, 182. FamilySearch records indicate Anna Buffington Waller was born in Topsfield, Massachusetts, in 1740, four years before Asael Smith, and three years before Mary Duty, and married Israel Waller in Topsfield on March 1, 1761. The Buffington family was connected to Asael Smith's Gould relatives by marriage. William Cutter, however, claims Anna Buffington was "of Fall River," Massachusetts, but gives no birth location; see William Richard Cutter, *New England Families: Genealogical and Memorial* (New York: Lewis Historical Publishing Company, 1914), 963; Lovejoy also suggests Anna was of Fall River, *History of Royalton*, 1013–1014. She may have moved to Fall River from Topsfield before moving again to Royalton, Vermont.

3. When a member of the Army Corp of Engineers evaluated the property, he officially designated it a fen, Scott Beavers, Personal Communication, October 2016.

4. Sidney Perley, ed., "Ipswich Court Records and Files," *The Essex Antiquarian* 11, no. 1, (January 1907), 22.

5. "John Smith's 1839 Recollections," in Richard Lloyd Anderson, *Joseph Smith's New England Heritage: Influences of Grandfathers Solomon Mack and Asael Smith*, Revised Edition (Provo, Utah: BYU Press, 2003), 191–193.

6. Between October 18–24, 2016 the authors visited the Smith farm in Topsfield, Massachusetts, along Pye Brook. At that time the land still had reeds and marsh grass growing in the low field behind the ridge where the Smith house had been located. The outline of a now missing barn/cooper shop was still visible in the grass above the fen and there was evidence of flooding along the brook across the entire area that had once been Smith property. Town residents noted the flooding was less significant now than it had been in their youth sixty years earlier and in centuries beforehand. See, George Francis Dow, *Town Records of Topsfield, Massachusetts, 1659-1778* (Topsfield, Mass.: Topsfield Historical Society, 1920), 1:vii-viii. Sidney Perley, *The History of Boxford, Essex County, Massachusetts* (Boxford, Mass.: Sidney Perley, 1880), 12–13, 24–25, 33–35, 40-42, and 54. Edward Johnson, "The Wonder-Working Providence of Sion's Saviour in New England, London, 1654," in George Francis Dow, ed., *Two Centuries of Travel in Essex County Massachusetts: A Collection of Narratives and Observations Made by Travelers, 1605-1799* (Topsfield, Mass.: The Topsfield Historical Society, 1921), 21.

7. Joseph Smith Sr.'s 100 acres in Manchester and his son Hyrum Smith's 80 acres adjacent to it in Palmyra, New York, include substantial wetlands on the western side of the property that were dried out over the years as later landowners dredged and straightened Crooked Creek. The woodlands in this area are currently being restored, although the creek cannot be given its earlier meandering path. White oak and ash trees suitable for making barrels grow well in these wetter areas and it is possible they were selected as ideal stands of trees for Hyrum Smith's coopering business rather than for grass growing potential. But grass may have been a bonus.

8. Jerry Kill, Personal Communication, August 10, 2017. Jerry Kill grew up on a dairy farm in Strafford Township and ran his own dairy farms at various locations for more than fifty years, including one in Tunbridge on part of what had been the Stephen Mack property where his wife Miriam Pease Kill grew up. They also operated a dairy farm together in Norwich, Vermont, on the farm Joseph and Lucy Smith rented from Squire Murdock. We are grateful for the patient teaching of Jerry and Miriam Kill in helping us understand many aspects of dairy farming in Orange County, Vermont, today.

9. Nick Bunker, *Making Haste from Babylon: The Mayflower Pilgrims and Their World* (New York: Alfred A. Knopf, 2010), 398.

10. Lovejoy, *History of Royalton*, 69.

11. Joseph F. Smith, Jr., "Asahel Smith of Topsfield, with Some Account of the Smith Family," *Topsfield Historical Collections* (Topsfield, Mass.: Topsfield Historical Society, 1902), 8:96.

12. Asael Smith's great-great grandson Joseph Fielding Smith took the name as offensive and as "applied to him by his opposers," and he offered the defense that the burn only made Asael's neck "stiff." Smith, "Asahel Smith of Topsfield, with Some Account of the Smith Family," 90. But he may have come to his conclusion without examining the name closely. Cleaveland said of Asael Smith, "This man, like 'Ammon's great son, one shoulder had too high." Cleaveland was citing a phrase from Alexander Pope's poem "Epistle to Dr. Arbuthnot" where Pope was describing himself. Pope believed his neck was slightly inclined towards his left shoulder, and playfully laughed at himself. Nehemiah Cleaveland, *An Address, Delivered at Topsfield in Massachusetts, August 28, 1850: The Two Hundredth Anniversary of the Incorporation of the Town* (New York: Pudney & Russell, 1851), XXV; John Wilson Croker, *The Works of Alexander Pope*, (London: John Murray, 1881), 3:250, see especially the footnotes. Most people had some kind of distinctive physical characteristic in the late eighteenth century, and given Asael Smith's sharp sense of humor and biting sarcasm, it is possible he gave the name to himself. For examples of both humor and sarcasm, see Anderson, *Joseph Smith's New England Heritage*, 125, 127.

13. Asael Smith paid 520 shillings for his land or 6,240 pence. See, "Elias Stevens to Asael Smith, June 21, 1791, Transfer of Deed," Tunbridge Deed Book A:324. See also, Elias Stevens to Peter Whitney, October 22, 1790, Tunbridge Deed Book A:269. Figuring out what money equivalencies were and how these related to income and family finances are part of "one of the most intractable problems a historian faces." John Steele Gordon, "The Problem of Money and Time," *American Heritage* 40, no. 4 (May/June, 1989), 57. John J. McCusker, in *How Much Is That in Real Money? A Historical Price Index for Use as a Deflator of Money Values in the Economy of the United States*, Second Edition (Worcester: American Antiquarian Society, 2001), 32–35, 52–53, 76–79, includes comprehensive tables on exchange rates between state issued Pounds, American Continentals, and British Pounds Sterling. He also provides a commodity price index that is helpful in assessing comparative purchasing power. We've used his valuation of four shillings and 6 pence per dollar, 4S 6d=$1, to give dollar figures for pounds, but recognize the exchange rate between states would mean dollars were purchased for different pound rates depending on where they were acquired.

14. McCusker, *How Much Is That in Real Money?*, 33-36.

15. Vermont set its exchange rate at 6 shillings per one-dollar in Spanish silver. Edward Day Collins, *A History of Vermont with the State Constitution, Geological, and Geographical Notes, Bibliography, Chronology, Statistical Tables, Maps, and Illustrations*,

Revised Edition (Boston: Ginn and Company, 1916), 158–160. We have reset these figures into British Sterling equivalencies.

16. McCusker notes that values of British pounds per dollar remained fairly stable through time, and he gives the equivalency as 4s 6d per dollar. We have determined an equivalency per £100 British sterling based on his figures, see McCusker, *How Much Is That in Real Money?*, 33.

17. A teacher's salary was set in 1804 for Sarah Flynn, and the salary to induce Mr. Tullar to settle as minister was set in 1779 at 50 pounds but steadily increased until it reached a maximum of 85 pounds. This salary was not paid in cash but in the house he was provided and the firewood and food he was given. The Smith property was also worth one bushel of wheat per each acre purchased since wheat sold in Royalton for 5 or 6 shillings a bushel, Lovejoy, *History of Royalton*, 196–197, 199, 288.

18. Asael Smith's son Jesse records transactions for the family's cooperage, including those of Asael Smith Jr., John Smith, and Silas Smith, with some trading with Joseph Smith Sr. Although Jesse's ledger was kept a decade after the family acquired their property, it confirms the high skill level of the family's cooperage activities noting his long-distance traveling selling wash tubs, kegs, and wet barrels as part of the family offerings, see Jesse Smith Ledger, 1807–1839; 1852–1865, MS 21878, Church History Library, the Church of Jesus Christ of Latter-day Saints, Salt Lake City, Utah (hereafter Church History Library). See data on coopers, schoolteachers, and ministers for the 1790-1810 period, Bureau of Labor Statistics, *History of Wages in the United States from Colonial Times to 1928* (Washington, DC: United States Government Printing Office, 1934), 11, 102, 130.

19. "John Smith's 1839 Recollections," 191. John suggests they were renting the cows in his account, and his father famously responded to the tax assessor in Topsfield in verse a few years earlier that he only owned three cows over four years of age. Ibid. 125.

20. For typical dairy sizes, see, Joan M. Jensen, *Loosening the Bonds: Mid-Atlantic Farm Women, 1750-1850* (New Haven: Yale University, 1986), 80-82, 86, 91-99; see also Lucy Diantha Morley Allen, "Autobiographical Sketch," n.p., Morley Family Histories. MS 6106, Church History Library; "Cows," Ohio Star 1, no. 19 (May 12, 1830): 1; and Portage County Tax Records, 1832, 114, Portage County Offices, Ravenna, Ohio.

21. Deborah Valenze, "The Art of Women and the Business of Men: Women's Work and the Dairy Industry C. 1740–1840," *Past & Present* 130, no.1 (February 1991), 143.

22. When William Marshall published his widely read book on dairy operations in 1787, he acknowledged the difficulty of getting good information on dairying from women. They controlled the "dairyroom," he argued, and "it is generally understood to require some interest, and more address, to gain full admission to its rites." William Marshall, *Rural Economy of Gloucestershire, including its Dairy: Together with the Dairy Management of North Wiltshire, and the Management of Orchards and Fruit Liquor, in Herefordshire*, 2nd Edition, 2 vols (London: G. Nicol Bookseller, 1796), 2:185. The book sold so well in both England and the United States that it was reprinted in 1796 and had a significant impact on dairy operation during the period of Smith family dairying. In a time when strict division of labor based on gender ruled, a father such as Asael who hoped to have a dairy was so dependent on daughters to work as dairymaids that "the misfortune of having only sons could force him into livestock farming instead of dairying" which could hamper the family's ability to make enough to meet payments. Valenze, "The Art of Women and the Business of Men," 147. Since Mary and her daughters controlled aspects of this knowledge, they certainly had some input in what the family concluded they could afford for land and possibly suggested specific details of their needs. When writer Mary Ann Evans (as George Eliot) described a 1799 English dairy family in her novel *Adam Bede*, she observed, "the woman who manages a dairy has a large share in making the rent." George Eliot, *Adam Bede* (London: William Blackwood and Sons, 1859), 2:25. Scholars have concluded her assessment was accurate for dairywomen and rent in general. Valenze, "The Art of Women and the Business of Men," 145.

23. For comparative data on milk, butter, and cheese prices in major urban centers, see Bureau of Labor Statistics, *History of Wages in the United States from Colonial Times to 1928* (Washington, D.C.: U.S. Government Printing Office, 1966). This data does not include information on Vermont dairies. But we have approximated Smith women earnings based on what they would have earned at their Massachusetts dairy. Boston sold dairy products for less than New York and Charleston. Butter was selling in Salem, Massachusetts, for one shilling to one shilling two pence a firkin. After the Smiths moved to Vermont, they could ship butter down the Connecticut River to New York for higher earnings, but it would still have been less than the retail price of butter in Salem. This also brought higher transportation costs and so the net profit was likely similar. Richard Lang, Jesse Smith's wholesaler for his store goods, bought local butter and shipped it to Salem. He was told that George Woodward's butter would not sell and was "very rank" and "any Butter put into such poor crocks as his, would soon spoile" (sic); but the Langs were able to sell Vermont cheese in Salem for from five to seven pence each. "Dr. Bro.r Salem 6 Sep.t 1797," and "Dr. Bro., Salem 2 Nov.r 1796," Richard Lang Papers 1983.003, box 1, folder 3B, New Hampshire Historical Society, Concord, New Hampshire. Cheese was consistently shipped and tracked in hogshead units. "Dear Bro., Hanover 1 Nov. 1798," Richard Lang Papers, Box 1, Folder 5. But it apparently was priced by the hundred pounds. The following year the Langs were buying cheese wholesale at nine dollars

per hundred pounds. "Dear Bro., Salem Octo.r 4th 1798 Thursday Eveng," Richard Lang Papers, Box 1, Folder 5.

24. "Elias Stevens to Asael Smith, June 21, 1791 Transfer of Deed," Tunbridge Deed Book, A: 324. *John Smith's 1839 Recollections*, 191 Jesse Smith later served as a witness when Asael Smith sold the land to James Adams, "Asael Smith to James Adams, April 29, 1805," Tunbridge Deed Book, 3: 282. It is unusual for Marsh to have served both as Justice of the Peace and as witness, and there was no legal justification for Jesse not filling that role, since when Stevens sold Peter Whitney two neighboring lots in the gore the previous fall, Whitney's sons Jonathan and Thomas served as witnesses for the transaction. Elias Stevens to Peter Whitney October 22, 1790, Tunbridge Deed Book, A:269. Although coverture laws gave Elias Stevens (and Asael Smith) all rights to family property, men could not sell the property without their wives signing over their widow's rights to one-third of the land. Elias Stevens's wife did not sign the deed. And although the land would become pasture for a dairy and primarily serve as Mary Smith's source of income, Mary did not sign over her rights later when Asael sold the land. Had Stevens wife later challenged the deed in court, the Smiths could have lost their land, but this was apparently a reflection of their lack of understanding of the law, and it was never challenged or rectified in the deeds. The laws were in force in Vermont when Asael Smith bought the property. It was usually the buyer's responsibility to insist that he get the wife's signature on the deed to assure the transfer could not later be contested. Gordon Madsen, Personal Communication, May 15, 2018. Later transfers of the property did include both signatures. Coverture laws were applicable when the Smiths acquired their land, and the lack of a signature suggests Asael Smith had little if any experience buying and selling land as he had rented property for most of his life. See, Richard H. Chused, "Married Women's Property and Inheritance by Widows in Massachusetts: A Study of Wills Probated between 1800 and 1850," *Berkeley Journal of Gender, Law & Justice* 2, no.1 (September 2013): 42–88; and Allison Anna Tait, "The Beginning of the End of Coverture: A Reappraisal of the Married Woman's Separate Estate," *Yale Journal of Law & Feminism* 26, no. 2, (2014): 165–216.

Chapter Three: The Smith Farm

1. The elevations were determined using GPS coordinates taken at the northeast corner of the Smith home during archeology and running an elevation line using Google Earth Pro through that point to the east and west boundary lines for the property. The highest point was determined using the east boundary line and following an elevation profile to the highest point on that boundary.

2. This location is known as Ward Hill Cemetery today.

3. See Americus K. and Jane (Adams) Howard to John Moxley for $1,300, 13 September 1854, Tunbridge Deed Book, 13:305. Fred Green, who has lived for 70 years on part of the Asael and Mary Duty Smith property in lot 10, recalled growing up with the understanding that the homesite near his had once had running water, Fred Green, Personal Communication, August 2017.

4. Ray Young, Personal Communication, August 2017.

5. Lovejoy, *History of Royalton*, 1014.

6. William Coxe, Esq., *A View of the Cultivation of Fruit Trees, and the Management of Orchards and Cider* (Philadelphia: M. Carey and Son, 1817), 106, indicates a resident of Burlington, Vermont, Samuel Allinson, gave the apple its name Maiden's Blush, but it is known by other names as well, and it is likely Allinson did not introduce the variety. Coxe notes, "the fruit ripens in August, and continues in perfection till the end of September, and is fit both for pies and the table." It was grown at least before 1800 and probably much earlier. This variety was soon introduced into the southern states and was a popular nineteenth-century variety in most of the United States, Creighton Lee Calhoun, Jr., *Old Southern Apples: A Comprehensive History and Description of Varieties for Collectors, Growers, and fruit Enthusiasts* (White River Junction, Vermont: Chelsea Green Publishing, 2010), 107.

7. Jesse Smith, Ledger, January 1808.

8. We are grateful to Ezekiel (Zeke) Goodband, the apple grower at Scott Farm in Dummerston, Vermont, for identifying this variety.

9. Essex Agricultural Society, Transactions of the Essex Agricultural Society for 1847 (Danvers, Mass.: Essex Agricultural Society, 1847), 125.

10. Ray Young and Evelyn Sargent both can remember fields of cows on the hillsides when they were very young. The east hill has been growing timber for seventy years, but the west hill has had pasturage and cows as recent as forty years ago.

11. Jerry Kill, Personal Communication, August 10, 2017.

12. These measurements are given using Google Earth's ruler and 1992 photographs based on information gathered during the 2017 walk of the property.

13. See Wessels, *Reading the Forested Landscape*, 44; and Wessels *Forest Forensics*, 99–101.

14. Joseph Smith Sr.'s New York neighbor Peter Ingersoll later suggested Smith told him "the heat of the sun caused the chests of money to rise to the top of the ground. You notice, said he, the large stones on the top of the ground—we call them rocks, and they truly appear so, but they are, in fact, most of them chests of money raised by the heat of the sun." Peter Ingersoll, "Affidavit," *Mormonism Unvailed*, E.D. Howe, ed. (Painesville: E. D. Howe, 1834), 233.

15. Porter Perrin, "Diary of a Vermont Farmboy, 1874," Vermont Historical Society.

16. Wessels includes photographs of these kinds of fences in his study of the phenomenon. See, Tom Wessels, *Forest Forensics: A Field Guide to Reading the Forested Landscape*, (Woodstock, Vermont: The Countryman Press, 2010), 32–33.

17. When trees fall in the woods, pulling their root balls out of the ground, they leave large holes. As the root balls slowly decay on the edge of the hole, the dirt from the balls fall in piles beside the holes. These holes are called cradles and the dirt piles are call pillows. While most of our experience working with the forested landscape comes through working closely over many years with Bob Parrott, caretaker for the Sacred Grove on the Smith property in Manchester, New York, several arborists have described old growth forests. One that particularly addresses learning details about early occupation from signs in the surviving landscape is Wessels. See Tom Wessels' books, *Reading the Forested Landscape: A Natural History of New England* (Woodstock, Vermont: The Countryman Press, 1997), and *Forest Forensics*. He acknowledges drawing on the research of Harvard naturalist Neil Jorgensen, *A Guide to New England's Landscape* (Barre, Mass.: Barre Publishers, 1971).

18. Wessels, *Reading the Forested Landscape*, 34–63. See also, Jorgensen, *A Guide to New England's Landscape*, 102, 233.

19. Ray Young, who lives southwest of the meadow, still remembers cows grazing on the west hillside 70 years ago (Personal Communication, August 2017). The trees on the east hill were clear cut by lumbermen about 50 years ago, and then again 20 years ago. The forest that currently grows on the hillside has grown rapidly. But the evidence of cattle on the hill in the nineteenth century is still clear. Because the pillows and cradles on the hillside have been plowed down but not obliterated, the hill has been used as pasture for a significant part of its history.

20. As dairyman Jerry Kill walked across the fen, he concluded only the smaller Jersey cows could negotiate the wet land well. Jerry Kill, Personal Communication, August 16, 2017. The Billings Farm and Museum staff in Woodstock, Vermont, not far from the Smith dairy, raise and interpret Jersey cows as the breed of choice for early Vermont settlers, Personal Communication, March 12, 2018.

21. Lucy Mack Smith, History, 1845, page 38, http://www.josephsmithpapers.org/paper-summary/lucy-mack-smith-history-1845/45. George A. Smith, was apparently the source of another historical account using similar language, saying: "At his marriage he owned a handsome farm in Tunbridge" (see Dan Vogel, ed., *History of Joseph Smith and The Church of Jesus Christ of Latter-day Saints: A Source—and Text—Critical Edition, 1839–1842*, (Salt Lake City: The Smith-Pettit Foundation, 2015), 4:181–182. It is probable that Lucy had used this same language more than once when telling others about her marriage and her husband's farm.

22. Silvanus Hayward, *History of the Town of Gilsum, New Hampshire, from 1752 to 1879* (Manchester, N.H.: John E. Clarke, 1881), 216. The two sisters, Lydia and Lucy, had a good relationship and Lydia named a daughter Lucy Bill. Samuel and Lydia Mack Bill's children were Samuel III, Eunice, Lydia Jr., Lucy, and David. David was born in 1794 and died that same year, two years before Lucy and Joseph Smith married. Hayward, *History of the Town of Gilsum*, 357, 265-266. Hayward lists Lucy Bill as dying in infancy, but FamilySearch lists her as marrying and having a family in Windsor County, Vermont, a few miles from where Lucy and Joseph lived. Samuel Bill and Lydia Mack Family, FamilySearch.org. Little Lucy Bill would have been four years old when Lucy Mack married Joseph Smith.

23. Lavina Fielding Anderson, ed., *Lucy's Book: A Critical Edition of Lucy Mack Smith's Family Memoir* (Salt Lake City: Signature Books, 2001), 247.

24. A story developed during the late twentieth century that Lucy Mack met Joseph Smith while clerking in her brother's store. There is no documentary evidence supporting this. And women at that time did not clerk in stores. Stephen Mack ran a textile mill and Lucy later noted she had "considerable" experience painting textiles (Anderson, *Lucy's Book*, 318). Lucy may have helped in textile production as well as working in the Mack tavern. The tavern would have included a kitchen, and Stephen's wife Temperance, a good friend of Lucy's, would have supervised several women who cooked, served, and cleaned up after customers. She was expecting twins when Lucy moved to her house, and it's likely Lucy was brought to help Temperance. See Mark Staker's class notes for Phil Dunning's course, "American Taverns, 1790–1840," Eastfield Village, Nassau, New York, June 2011, author's files.

25. When the Smith family arrives in Palmyra, they turn immediately to selling beer and other refreshments using a makeshift handcart and a stationary booth. Their store sold "gingerbread, pies, boiled eggs, root-beer, and other like notion." They continued to peddle "cake and beer" after they moved to Manchester. See Pomeroy Tucker, *Origin, Rise, and Progress of Mormonism: Biography of Its Founders and History of Its Church* (New York: D. Appleton and Company, 1867), 12, 14; and, Thomas L. Cook, *Palmyra and Vicinity* (Palmyra, New York: The Palmyra Courier-Journal, 1930), 219.

26. Lucy Mack Smith, History, 1845, 247, 282. Joseph Smith Jr. purchased the tavern from A. Sidney Gilbert and later gave it to his parents to operate. Thanks to Jenny Reader for pointing out Lucy's tavern experience in Missouri.

27. See Robert Smith of Boxford, Probate Record January 2, 1698, Old Series Probate, Essex County, Massachusetts, vols. 304–306. 1683–1699; and Samuel Smith of Topsfield, Probate Record August 22, 1748, Old Series Probate, Essex County, Massachusetts, vol. 328, 115–116; and "Suffolk County Deeds," *The Essex Antiquarian* 9, no. 3 (July 1905), 149-150; Albert Harrison Hoyt, ed., *New England Historic, Genealogical Society* (Boston: David Clapp and Son, 1873), 27: 149-150; and Henry F. Waters, *Genealogical Gleanings in England* (Boston: New England Historic Genealogical Society, 1901), 424-425. Lucy's father made his living building dams and bridges. Hayward, *History of the Town of Gilsum*, 53–55, 58, 136, 204, 432.

28. Although almost all early American families pursued some kind of agricultural activity on the side (Richard Lyman Bushman, *The American Farmer in the Eighteenth Century: A Social and Cultural History* (New Haven: Yale University Press, 2018), 9-12), the Smith choice of cattle as their side operation influenced their selection of land, how they organized their landscape, and the focus of their efforts on the land. Cattle clearly took priority over other agricultural pursuits.

29. See the Richard Lang Papers, box 4, folder 5B. Lucy Smith's autobiography, http://www.josephsmithpapers.org/paper-summary/lucy-mack-smith-history-1844-1845/21. Moxley, 1800 U.S. Census Records, Randolph Township, Orange County, Vermont. Childs, *Gazetteer of Orange County*, 158-160.

30. Euclid Farnham, Tunbridge Town Historian, Personal Communication, October 29, 2016.

31. Adam Krakowski, "A Bitter Past: Hop Farming in Nineteenth-Century Vermont," *Vermont History* 82, no. 2 (Summer/Fall 2014), 103. By 1800 New Englanders drank 35 gallons of beer a year per person—that's twelve ounces a day for every man, woman, and child, Adam Krakowski, "Vermont's Long Thirst for Good Brew," *Burlington Free Press* June 12, 2015, 3. Although Krakowski argues New Englanders drank seven glasses of beer a day per person, the math suggests he meant to write seven glasses a week. Joseph and Lucy Smith's Puritan ancestors sailed to America in ships filled with barrels of beer. David Hackett Fischer, *Albion's Seed: Four British Folkways in America* (Oxford: Oxford University Press, 1989), 137; George Francis Dow, *Every Day Life in the Massachusetts Bay Colony* (Boston: Society for the Preservation of New England Antiquities, 1935), 84, 89. For a brief period in the nineteenth century Vermont took the lead in New England hop production. Krakowski, "A Bitter Past," 91–105. Kurt Staudter and Adam Krakowski, *Vermont Beer: History of a Brewing Revolution* (Charleston, S.C.: American Palate, 2014), 16–17. Beer production be-

gan in Vermont as early as 1776, (see Abby Maria Hemenway, ed., *The Vermont Historical Gazetteer: A Magazine, Embracing a History of Each Town* (Burlington, Vt.: A. M. Hemenway, 1867) 1:514–515, 860, 873). Jabez Rogers opened a brewery in Middlebury in 1792. William Guthrie, *A New System of Modern* Geography (Philadelphia: Matthew Carey,1795), 331. By 1799 Vermont newspapers published instructions for farmers on properly harvesting hops. "To Farmers," *Federal Galaxy* [Brattleboro, Vermont], September 23, 1799, 4. Beer was considered healthy and sociable. Vermont newspapers promised readers a range of health benefits, including that "Those who drink freely of hop beer will not be troubled with jaundice or dysentery." "The Hop," *The Green Mountain Patriot* 8, no.397 (September 24, 1805), 1. Newspapers encouraged regular hop beer drinking as "not only wholesome and palatable, but of great utility in repressing the root of the odious and impoverishing vice, drunkenness," since everyone drank alcohol and drinking water was often the source of illness in a family. A Friend to Malt Liquor, "Husbandry," *Green Mountain Patriot* April 27, 1803, 4. Hops were also a major source of yeast. Any housewife planning to bake bread had to keep a start from earlier dough or beer production in a dark corner of her pantry unless she had access to hops. Virginia Grosvenor Alee, *All About Grandmother Grosvenor's 1827 Cookbook* (Boulder, Colorado, Virginia Alee, 1981), 64, 69, 147–149, 265. See also "The Hungarian Art of Making Excellent Bread without Yeast," *Philadelphia Magazine and Review*, February 28, 1799, 29. Even "refuse" hops, those flowers not reaching first or second quality, turned out to be ideal as a yeast starter for sourdough bread or as pig feed, so there was a ready market for all grades of the flowers.

32. Hillside hop yards tended to ripen hops a few days later in the season than valley hop yards. See Albert C. Bullard, *The Hop Farmer's Year: The Seasons, Tools and Methods of Hop Growers in New York State's Golden Age of Hops* (Schenectady, New York: Square Circle Press, 2015), 58.

33. Hop growers were encouraged to lay their soil up in high ridges to keep the hop roots dry. The hillsides of the Smith farm were good ways to accomplish the same task without all the extra labor. See, Amana, "Culture of Hops: of the Proper Land for Hop Ground," *Vermont Intelligencer* August 4, 1817, 1. Scott and Patricia Beavers currently grow hops as part of their large garden on the Smith property.

34. Bullard, *The Hop Farmer's Year*, 8.

35. Hannah Glasse, *The Art of Cookery Made Plain and Easy* (Alexandria: Cottom and Stewart, 1805), 195–198. Grosvenor's 1827 cookbook from Geneva, New York, includes a recipe for "Ginger Beer" that builds on using the "best ginger" and sugar with cream of tartar and lemon. An 1832 recipe calls for Seville orange peel instead of lemon. Although Grosvenor's recipe does not include hops as an independent ingredient in her ginger beer, it is the main ingredient in her recipe for yeast. And she

recommends yeast in her ginger beer (see Allee, *All About Grandmother Grosvenor's 1827 Cookbook*, 152, 265. Grosvenor recommends molasses for her sugar, but maple sugar could be easily used instead. By 1851 in Royalton citizens tried to control vendors selling cakes, pies, small beer, and cider and required they be licensed (Lovejoy, *History of Royalton*, 599).

36. L.L. Dutcher, "June Training in Vermont," in Hemenway, ed., *The Vermont Historical Gazetteer*, 2:347, 356.

37. Pomeroy Tucker, *Origin, Rise, and Progress of Mormonism: Biography of Its Founders and History of Its Church* (New York: D. Appleton and Company, 1867), 12, 14; and, Thomas L. Cook, *Palmyra and Vicinity* (Palmyra, New York: The Palmyra Courier-Journal, 1930), 219.

38. Tucker, *Origin, Rise and Progress of Mormonism*, 12.

39. Child, *Gazetteer of Orange County, Vermont, 1762–1888*, 344.

40. William Goodwin, "Wanted, by the Subscriber," *Green Mountain Patriot* [Peacham, Vermont], June 18, 1800, 3. Even in 1850, after prohibition was well underway in Vermont and most counties had already outlawed alcohol, but before Vermont would become dry statewide in 1853, George Peterson was still producing 500 barrels of beer using 2,000 pounds of hops a year. U.S. Department of Agriculture, "Seventh Census of the United States original returns of the assistant marshals: fourth series: manufacturing production by counties: 1850". Microfilm 626, Reel 2. Bailey/Howe Microforms, University of Vermont: Burlington.

41. "Prices Current," *Pennsylvania Magazine* March 31, 1798, 51.

42. Krakowski, "A Bitter Past," 93.

43. Bullard, *The Hop Farmer's Year*, 8–9.

44. A natural fen preserves plant pollen well and a careful pollen analysis done with residue in the Smith meadow could recover hop pollen or pollens of other plants grown in the area.

Chapter Four: The Smith Log Cabin

1. "*John Smith's 1839 Recollections*," 194; text corrections based on comparisons with the original manuscript, John Smith, Autobiography, July 20, 1839, n.p., in Journal 1833–1841, MS 1326 John Smith papers, 1833–1854, MS 1326 Box 1, folder 1, Church History Library.

2. Elias Smith, *The Life, Conversion, Preaching, Travels, and Sufferings of Elias Smith* (Portsmouth, New Hampshire: Beck & Foster, 1816), 36–37.

3. See Harold R. Shurtleff, *The Log Cabin Myth: A Study of the Early Dwellings of the English Colonists in North America* (Gloucester, Mass.: Peter Smith, 1967), 209–212; and, C. A. Weslager, *The Log Cabin in America: From Pioneer Days to the Present* (New Brunswick, NJ: Rutgers University Press, 1969), 116–132, especially 121–122.

4. Nash, *The Town of Royalton*, 109.

5. For other references to bark roofs in Tunbridge, see Hemenway, ed., *The Vermont Historical Gazetteer* 2:1116. Illustration of a bark roof held down with rails is from Orsamus Turner, *Pioneer History of the Holland Purchase of Western New York* (Buffalo: Jewett, Thomas & Co., 1849), 564.

6. Lovejoy, *History of Royalton*, 151. Hemenway, ed., *The Vermont Historical Gazetteer* 2:1119.

7. Hemenway, ed., *The Vermont Historical Gazetteer*, 2:1115, 1119.

8. Lovejoy, *History of Royalton*, 293, 350, 357, 514-515. Michael Williams, *Americans and their Forests: a historical geography* (Cambridge: Cambridge University Press, 1992), 68.

9. O. S. Morris, "Tunbridge," in Hemenway, ed., *The Vermont Historical Gazetteer*, 1119.

10. Silas McKeen, *A History of Bradford, Vermont* (Montpelier, Vermont: J. D. Clark & Son, 1875), 283; Amos Churchill, "Hubbardton," in Abby Maria Hemenway, ed., *The History of Rutland County, Vermont* (White River Junction, Vermont: White River Paper Co., 1882), 751. Franklin Ellis describes settlers in western New York who came from Vermont and built "a shanty of logs." One side was eight feet high and the other was six feet, and the bark was laid on top, held down by poles tied to the rafters, Franklin Ellis, *History of Cattaraugus Co., New York* (Philadelphia: L. H. Everts, 1879), 285.

11. *John Smith's 1839 Recollections*, 194.

12. See Jesse Smith to Benjamin Peabody, January 15, 1796, Tunbridge Deed Book 2:168.

13. Peabody also made his own barrels as well as coffins, and he owned a cider mill where settlers brought their apples and could leave with cider in his barrels. Benjamin Peabody Account Book, 1784–1810, MSS 1293.2, Phillips Library, Peabody Essex Museum, Salem, Massachusetts, see entries for Eleazer Brown, February 21,

1789; April 8, 1789; April 27, 1789; October 14, 1789; November 14 & 16, 1789; December 2, 1789; September 17, 1790, August 28, 1793.

14. Jane C. Nylander, *Our Own Snug Fireside: Images of the New England Home, 1760–1860* (New Haven: Yale University Press, 1993), 20–23, 54–62.

15. The deed was recorded a few days later. Asael Smith from Lois Botton, 2 December 1794, Tunbridge Deed Book 2:121.

16. Asael Smith from Hezekiah Hutchinson, 23 December 1795, Tunbridge Deed Book 2:211.

17. "Asahel Smith to Jacob Towne, Tunbridge, January 14, 1796," in "Town Family Papers" *The Historical Collections of the Topsfield Historical Society* vo. 18 (1913): 39–42.

18. "Asahel Smith to Jacob Towne, Tunbridge, January 14, 1796."

19. Benjamin Peabody from Jesse Smith, January 15, 1796, Tunbridge Deed Book 2:168.

20. Tunbridge Town Records, Tunbridge Town Clerk's office on page 129 (second numbering). "This may certify that Joseph Smith was married to Lucy Mack on the 24 of January AD 1796 by me attest Seth Austin Justice Peace, A true Record H Hutchinson T.C. [Town Clerk]"

21. Tunbridge Town Records, Tunbridge Town Clerk's office for March 13, 1798 on page 152 (second numbering). The survey notes read: "A survey of a Road beginning at the North East Corner of Asahel Smiths House thence S. 10 E. 26 Rods thence S. 40 E. 34 Rods thence S 32 E 40 Rods thence S. 88 E. 25 Rods thence N. 71 E. 20 Rods, thence S. 70 E. 22 Rods thence S. 79 E. 26 Rods thence N. 44 E. 54 Rods thence N. 17 E. 13 Rods thence N. 8 E 13 Rods thence N 21 E 13 Rods thence N. 33 E 17 Rods thence N. 35 E. 24 Rods thence N. 27 E. 68 Rods thence S 86 E 16 Rods thence N 41 E 52 Rods thence N. 22 E. 26 Rods thence N. 44 [42] E. 21 Rods thence N. 45 E. 24 Rods thence N. 83 E. 52 Rods thence N. 44 E. 11 Rods to the Road from Mr. Seth Paines to Randolph S.d [Said] Road Esctending [Extending] 3 Rods to the Right Hand Tunbridge March 13, 1798 Elijah Tracy County Surveyor Received for Record attyst. H. Hutchinson T. Clerk."
This survey was retraced by the authors to confirm the original house corner based on a quadrant bearing system with the bearing measured as an angle from the reference meridian (in this case south was 0 degrees) toward the east or west. Measurements were made using a smartphone compass and 50' tape measure. Because part of the road was abandoned well over a century ago, segments of the road were confirmed using aerial photographs and Google Earth imagery. For details about Jigger Village, see Daniel Tarbell, *Incidents of Real Life* (Montpelier: Argus, 1883),

25. See also "Oren Burbank Diary" in Nash, *Royalton, Vermont*, 37; and Farnham, *Tunbridge Past*, 70.

22. George Albert Smith's diary that records his tour of church history sites in 1907 does not mention visiting the site. But he spent two days in the South Royalton, Sharon, Tunbridge area, and on June 20, 1907, he recorded in his diary on page 189 "I took some snap shots this AM." That afternoon he left Vermont. See George Albert Smith diary vol 1, 1890 May–1891 November and 1903 October–1908 November, MS 8266 Church History Library.

23. Evelyn Sargent with Ray and Beverly Young, Personal Communications, August 12, 2017.

24. Larry E. Dahl, "Vermont," LaMar C. Berrett, ed., *Sacred Places, New England and Eastern Canada: A Comprehensive Guide to Early LDS Historical Sites* (Salt Lake City: Bookcraft, 1999), 113.

25. A Vermonter noting these abandoned cellars a century ago, later wrote: "My interest in migration from New England began some forty-years ago, when I first became conscious of the many deserted hill farms in my native Vermont, and in New Hampshire where I also lived. The old cellar holes, the orchards being slowly throttled by encroaching forest, moved me deeply. I had a fairly good idea of what had gone into the making of those hill farms and homes; and the fact that they had been abandoned, after a century or more, seemed to me to be a great tragedy. It still does." Stewart H. Holbrook, The Yankee Exodus: An Account of Migration from New England (Seattle: University of Washington Press, 1950), vii.

26. We laid out a grid beginning at the northeast corner with marker at Site #1 labeled S1 1A at point N 43° 52.313' W 072° 32.309, 1,213 feet elevation. We measured from powerline pole FP11 as a backup to the gps system, and the marker was 93 feet 7 inches 320° northwest of pole FP11. We placed marker S12 1A N43° 52.301 W072°32.303, sixty feet from the first marker at 1,215 feet elevation. The northwest corner at marker S1 1F measured 25 feet from S1 1A at point N43° 52.309 W 072° 32.317. We placed marker S12 1F at the southwest corner measuring exactly 60 feet from the northwest corner and 25 feet from the southeast corner. For detailed information about the grid, see Mark Staker's fieldnotes of the project.

27. Matthew Kirk, Hartgen Archaeological Associates, Renssellaer, New York, had his team of brick experts look at several fragments recovered from the site. They suggested the brick dated from 1750–1800. Kirk, Personal Communication, December 2016.

28. Some additional nineteenth- and twentieth-century artifacts were recovered from the edge of the site or on the surface before digging began that had been pushed into the site during road construction or left by visitors at later points. These include a mid-nineteenth-century pin and washer used to attach a plow or harrow to a single-tree. These were likely lost by a farmer moving equipment through the area on the road. A .30-06 bullet shell casing left by a hunter, and twentieth-century bottles and other refuse left on the surface, perhaps by early tourists visiting the site.

CHAPTER FIVE: Smith Family Comforts of Life

1. Nylander, *Our Own Snug Fireside*, 20–23, 54–62.

2. Frederick Tupper and Helen Tyler Brown, eds., *Grandmother Tyler's Book: the Recollections of Mary Palmer Tyler, 1775–1866* (New York: G. P. Putnam's Sons, 1925), 180.

3. Tupper and Brown, eds. *Grandmother Tyler's Book*, 217.

4. The Stephen and Temperance Mack Tunbridge House foundations have not yet been identified and excavated. Excavations of the Stephen Mack house in Winnebago County, Illinois, as part of the restoration of Macktown Historic District, were actually carried out at Stephen Mack Jr.'s residence built in 1839. See Robert A. Birmingham, "Historical Archaeological Investigations at the Stephen Mack House," Great Lakes Archaeological Research Center, November 25, 1981. Copy in possession of Mark Staker.

5. Anderson, ed., *Lucy's Book*, 275.

6. This spoon bowl was found by a visitor to the site a few days after we finished our archaeology of the neighboring property and was not part of our project. Since it was found on property of the Church of Jesus Christ of Latter-day Saints, the spoon is now catalogued in the collection of the Church History Museum in Salt Lake City, where it's available for research.

7. John D. Davis, *Pewter at Colonial Williamsburg* (Hanover, N.H.: University Press of New England, 2003), 165–183; David Moulson, "The Development of the Modern Spoon Shape," *Journal of the Pewter Society* 19, no. 4 (Autumn 1998): 6; Ronald F. Homer, *Five Centuries of Base Metal Spoons* (London: The Worshipful Company of Pewterers, 1975), 43–48; F. G. Hilton Price, *Old Base Metal Spoons with Illustrations and Marks* (London, 1908).

8. See Nylander, *Our Own Snug Fireside*, 59–60.

9. Brimsley Peabody Debits, November 26, 1799 "1 /2 & Runing 4. Spons /4"; and, Oct-21,1802. "To Casting six Puter spons 004," in Benjamin Peabody Account Book. A "running" is a series of castings out of the same mold, see N. Hudson Moore, *The Collector's Manual* (New York: Frederick A. Stokes Company, 1906), 275.

10. James Deetz, *In Small Things Forgotten: An Archaeology of Early American* Life (New York: Anchor Books, 1996), 172–173. Although Deetz sees a shift occurring to intentionally dug garbage pits mid-eighteenth century, it does not occur in Massachusetts or Vermont until well after that date.

11. Josiah Quincy, "An Address Delivered before the Massachusetts Agricultural Society, at the Brighton Cattle Show, October 12, 1819," *Massachusetts Agricultural Journal* 6, no. 1 (January 1820): 5.

12. George C. Neumann, *Early American Antique Country Furnishings: Northeastern America, 1650–1800s* (Gas City, Indiana: L-W Book Sales, 1996), 299.

13. Jack Larkin masterfully describes how this took place in rural Massachusetts in "From 'Country Mediocrity' to 'Rural Improvement': Transforming the Slovenly Countryside in Central Massachusetts, 1775–1840," in Catherine E. Hutchins, ed. *Everyday Life in the Early Republic* (Winterthur, Delaware: Henry Francis du Pont Winterthur Museum, 1994), 175–200.

14. Dating of queensware fragments provided by ceramics specialists at Hartgen Archaeological Associates in Renssellaer, New York, and confirmed by Don Enders through independent analysis.

15. O. S. Morris, "Tunbridge," in Hemenway, ed., *The Vermont Historical Gazetteer*, 2:1123. The Congregational Church membership later also paid for rum themselves to encourage additional community work on their building.

16. Benjamin Peabody Account Book, 1784–1810. Peabody also occasionally lists transactions for "sundries in the Rum Book." It appears these entries are about another account book kept separately for a rum business of some kind. The second book no longer survives.

17. See the discussion on rum and sugar by Jesse Smith's merchandise supplier Richard Lang with his brother Daniel Lang. "Dear Bro. Salem 23 July 1813, Richard Lang Papers, box 4, folder 5B.

18. See Staker, Notes from Phil Dunning's, "American Taverns, 1790–1840."

19. See Jacob Towne's Account Book for Topsfield, Massachusetts, expenses, "Town Family Papers" *The Historical Collections of the Topsfield Historical Society* vo. 18 (1913): 28, 31, and 33. Costs in Tunbridge would have only been slightly higher for the rum and lemons and slightly lower for the barrels and turnips. See also, Carroll D. Wright, *Comparative Wages, Prices, and Cost of Living* (Boston: Wright & Potter Printing Co., State Printers, 1889), 122–123.

20. See the Richard Lang Papers, box 4, folder 5B, where Lang mentions frequently in his correspondence boxes of lemons and barrels of rum going out to various merchants.

21. Hezekiah Hutchinson, Clerk, Tunbridge Township Records, April 27, 1793, 76.

22. Jesse Smith, Ledger, 1807–1839, entry for Joseph Smith [Sr.], 15 March 1808.Lucy Mack Smith gives the birthdate of her son Samuel Harrison as March 13, 1808, http://www.josephsmithpapers.org/paper-summary/lucy-mack-smith-history-1845/354#full-transcript.

23. George L. Miller and Robert Hunter, "How Creamware Got the Blues: The Origins of China Glaze and Pearlware," in Robert Hunter, ed., *Ceramics in America* (Hanover: University Press of New England, 2001), 135–161, especially, 157. See also, Ann Smart Martin, "Magical, Mythical, Practical, and Sublime: The Meanings and Uses of Ceramics in America," in Robert Hunter, ed., *Ceramics in America* (Hanover: University Press of New England, 2001), 32–39; and Lisa McAllister, *Collector's Guide to Feather Edge Ware: Identification and Values* (Paducah, KY: Collector Books, 2001). These plates could be used by family for many years after they were first made. Lucy's nephew Stephen Mack Jr. left behind fragments of a similar dinner platter at his Illinois home in the 1840s, see Birmingham, "Historical Archaeological Investigations at the Stephen Mack House," 36.

24. George L. Miller, Ann Smart Martin, and Nancy S. Dickinson, "Changing Consumption Patterns: English Ceramics and the American Market from 1770–1840," in Catherine E. Hutchins, ed., *Everyday Life in the Early Republic* (Winterthur, Delaware: Henry Francis du Pont Winterthur Museum, 1994), 222–224. We are grateful to George Miller, who was first introduced to early American ceramics while excavating historic sites in Nauvoo, Illinois, with Don Enders under the direction of J. C. Harrington and Virginia Harrington, for providing input and generously sharing his insights on ceramics over many years.

25. Miller, et al., "Changing Consumption Patterns," 222–224.

26. Diana and J. Garrison Stradling, "American Queensware—The Louisville Experience, 1829-1837," in Robert Hunter, ed., *Ceramics in America* (Hanover: University Press of New England, 2001), 176.

27. This date was confirmed independently by ceramics experts at Hartgen Archeological Associates. Matt Kirk, Vice President, Hartgen Archeological Associates, Rensselaer, New York, Personal Communication to Mark Staker, November 28, 2016.

28. Miller, et al., "Changing Consumption Patterns," 219–248.

29. We are grateful to Lindsay Johansson at the University of Colorado, Boulder for her careful osteology work and to Ryan Saltzgiver at the Church of Jesus Christ of Latter-day Saints History Department for facilitating the study. The shaft of the tibia was damaged in the mail when the items were shipped back to the authors after the dig, and it was glued back together for study.

CHAPTER SIX: A Smith Industrial Building

1. This feature was labeled Site #2 in our fieldnotes. Its northwest corner begins at 43°52'17.61"N latitude and 72°32'15.64"W longitude at an elevation of 1,143 feet.

2. The nails found at the Smith industrial site were all machine cut, and at least two of them had hand attached heads. Corrosion obscures the heads of the other two nails. The two hand attached heads were formed with special dies. The special lozenge or double countersink shaped head distinctive to animal shoes was formed by a blacksmith hitting the nail into a special die while still hot. William Moorcroft, *Cursory Account of the Various Methods of Shoeing Horses, Hitherto Practiced* (London: W. Bulmer and Company, 1800), 50, see also Edward Coleman, *Observations on the Structure, Economy, and Diseases of the Foot of the Horse, and on the Principles and Practices of Shoeing* (Dublin: Grosberg and Campbell, 1798), 88-90, and Plate 4 Figure 4. Although it is often assumed cut nails are an early nineteenth-century introduction, and William Adams argues in his masterful study of the history of wire nails that cut nails first came into wide use about 1815 (see William Hampton Adams, "Machine Cut Nails and Wire Nails: American Production and Use for Dating 19th-Century and Early-20th-Century Sites," *Historical Archaeology* 36, no.4 (2002), 66,) primary sources suggest they were commonly used a decade or two earlier. (We are grateful to Benjamin Pykles for helping us better understand the current view of nail dating in historic archaeology.) Jeremiah Wilkinson first introduced cold cut nails in Cumberland, Rhode Island, in 1777, and Jacob Perkins invented a nail-cutting machine in Newburyport, Massachusetts in 1790. Near the Smith Tunbridge residence ore mining began before 1785 in Rutland county. (James M. Swank, *History of the Manufacture of Iron in All Ages and Particularly in the*

United States from Colonial Times to 1891, also a Short History of Early Coal Mining in the United States (Philadelphia: Burt Franklin, 1892), 134, 133). Vermont desperately needed construction materials during the early settlement period. But in 1785 the State Legislature put a duty of two pence per pound on nails brought into Vermont to encourage local production. Matthew Lyon built a dam that year to turn his waterwheel for an iron manufactory at Fairhaven in Rutland County almost 63 miles west of Tunbridge using ore mined locally. He installed trip hammers turned rapidly by the waterwheels to cut nails from rolled sheets of iron after which he attached the nail heads by hand. By 1795 the Fairhaven ironworks was shipping kegs of these cut nails throughout the region. (see H.P. Smith and W. S. Rann, *History of Rutland County, Vermont* (Syracuse, N.Y.: D. Mason & Co.), 1886, 604, 881. See also pages 435, 671, 812, 864, and 892). The township just west of Tunbridge, Randolph, had two forges and a slitting machine in operation before 1800 (Swank, *History of the Manufacture of Iron*, 133). James Parton, Rayard Taylor, Amos Kendall, E D. May, and J. Alexander Patten, argue in *Sketches of Men of Progress* (New York: Greer and Company, 1870), 411, that Samuel Bement made wrought nails in Tunbridge Township because they assumed (relying on consensus at the time) cut nails had not yet been invented. Bement, however, leased a millrace to run his nail making operation and the lease specifically mentioned trip hammers—the equipment used to make cut nails. On January 2, 1795, Samuel Bement arrived in Tunbridge and began making cut nails. He built a nail factory on the river and used the milldam and waterways from Elias Curtis's gristmill. When Curtis leased his sawmill to Lucy's brother Stephen Mack in 1803, he renewed his lease to Bement to continue using water powered trip hammers to make nails. The lease does not indicate when Bement started making cut nails, but he quickly became a major distributor and would have needed lots of kegs to ship his nails throughout the state. See Elias Curtis and Samuel Bement Lease, April 5, 1803, Tunbridge Deed Book 3:58. Richard Lang, who supplied many of the merchants in Orange County, Vermont, notes in his request to a printer to publish a list of his merchandise, that he has "a constant supply of cut nails & brads" along with English and American wrought nails as well as iron and steel, "Copy of Advertizement," June 5, 1800," Richard Lang Papers, box 2, folder 1B. The Lang advertisement confirms cut nails were available to the Smiths at least as early as 1800. The physical evidence supports the documentary evidence. Tom Visser, Director of the Historic Preservation Program at the University of Vermont, has found cut nails in a 1789 Ferrisburgh, Vermont, home. Thomas Visser, Personal Communication, 13 June 2018. The research on the "old part" of the Robinson House (Rokeby Museum) in Ferrisburgh, Vermont, has not yet been published. But Visser has found L-headed cut nails in the Rueben Harmon Store in Burlington, Vermont, that were installed when the store was built in 1811. This research is included in the National Register nomination amendment available at https://www.burlingtonvt.gov/sites/default/files/PZ/Historic/National-Register-PDFs/WinooskiFallsHDAmendment.pdf. Visser agrees the cut nails found at the Smith farm site could date to as early as 1791, and so they do not exclude the outbuilding from being Asael and Mary Smith construction. The Smiths may have also been able to get cut nails in Salem, Massachusetts, without paying a duty if they did not sell them on the open market, see Maureen K. Phillips, "Mechanic Geniuses and Duckies Redux: Nail Makers and Their Machines," *The Journal of Preservation Technology* 27, no. 1-2 (1996), 47-56. The nails found on the Smith property are of the style Visser describes as a "Type A cut nail," and include a tapered shank. He dates this style to circa 1790–1830. Thomas Visser, *A Field Guide to New England Barns and Farm Buildings* (Hanover, N.H.: University Press of New England, 1997), 24. See also, Thomas D. Visser, "Nails: Clues to a Building's History," University of Vermont Historic Preservation Program, https://www.uvm.edu/~histpres/203/nails.html.

3. Krakowski, *A Bitter Past*, 98-99, documents an 1865 oast which was two stories high and had a large drying kiln on the main level. It is likely an 1800 kiln would be smaller in comparison. Remnants of a kiln would likely show up in a full excavation of the site if it had indeed been used as an oast.

4. Lucy Smith uses the term stable in her history as the place where they keep a horse. It would not have had any foundations at all, see Lucy Mack Smith, History, 1844-1845, book 16, page 7. http://www.josephsmithpapers.org/paper-summary/lucy-mack-smith-history-1844-1845/197.
She also recognizes a barn's typical feed storing role and notes a Mr. Osgood put their animals in his barn yard to keep them, not in a building, but he fed them from his barn. Lucy Mack Smith, History, 1845, page 188. http://www.josephsmithpapers.org/paper-summary/lucy-mack-smith-history-1845/188.

5. Bullard, *The Hop Farmer's Year*, 88–96.

6. M. G. Kains, *Ginseng: Its Cultivation, Harvesting, Marketing and Market Value, with a Short Account of Its History and Botany* (New Edition), New York: Orange Judd Company, 1903), 41–45. Putting ginseng in the sun to dry discolors it. The best conditions for drying ginseng are a low humidity place kept at about 90 degrees Fahrenheit. Valerie J. Davidson, Xiang Li, and Ralph B. Brown, "Forced-air Drying of Ginseng Roots: 2. Control Strategy for Three-Stage Drying Process," *Journal of Food Engineering* 63, no.4 (August 2004), 369–373.

7. https://www.josephsmithpapers.org/paper-summary/lucy-mack-smith-history-1845/49

Chapter Seven: Selling Smith Settlement

1. Evelyn Sargant, who lived for more than eighty years on the property Anderson photographed, remembers when the home burned down in 1961. Her family found lots of very old artifacts within the foundation when they rebuilt the house on its

original cellar. It had three large rooms on the main level and four rooms upstairs. The public road originally ran alongside the front of the house separating it from the well across the road until the road was moved to high ground more than a hundred feet west of the home. Evelyn Sargant, Personal Communication, August 12, 2017. Early photographs of the property and an examination of the site suggests a lot of details about Asael and Mary Smith's life there, but space does not allow for a discussion of the property in this article.

2. The small barn raised and attached to a larger barn as a loft to aid in lowering hay or grain into wagons is likely the original Smith barn. It is a good model for the size, shape, and character of a possible barn on the Joseph and Lucy Smith property.

3. See Andrew and Rachel Perkins to Benjamin Peabody and Asa How, March 28, 1807, Deed Book, Essex County 181:96. Michael David Scholl in *The American Yeoman: An Historical Ecology of Production in Colonial Pennsylvania* (Dissertation, University of North Carolina at Chapel Hill, 2008) has argued that although yeoman in 1776 meant farmer in the same way one might call themselves a baker, weaver, or carpenter, it also had a much deeper meaning that reflected class structure which developed during the Revolutionary War. Scholl shares data from tax records and other sources produced between 1760–1780 and argues during that period more men were identified as yeoman than farmer. He suggests the term yeoman took on deeper political meaning during the Revolutionary era as an effort to flatten class structure to further distinguish themselves from the Tories and the British culture and society they were rejecting. This brought "gentlemen landowners" who were wealthy more on the level of the working man or even the poor. While Scholl looked specifically at Pennsylvania and not Massachusetts, his study is suggestive of Peabody's use of "gentleman" to describe himself and yeoman to describe his business partners may have attempted to preserve the earlier distinctions. It clearly suggested he saw himself in a different category than the other men.

4. Although Benjamin Peabody "of Middleton" buys several Smith family properties, he never moves to Tunbridge and continues to do business in Middleton as a resident of that town (see Benjamin Peabody to Joshua Daniele, April 6, 1803, Deed Book, Essex County 171:232. Hannah Peabody Deposition June 30, 1803 Deed Book, Essex County 172:220, where 81-year-old Hannah Peabody testifies as about a case where she served as midwife May 7 or 9, 1741). Andrew Perkins and Rachel Perkins to Benjamin Peabody and Asa How March 28, 1807, Deed Book, Essex County181:96. Benjamin Peabody Account Book.

5. Benjamin Peabody from Jesse Smith, January 15, 1796, Tunbridge Deed Book 2:168.

6. There is no apparent record of this mortgage in the deed books, but it is later referenced and cancelled in Jesse Smith from Benjamin Peabody, 16 December 1799, Tunbridge Deed Book 2:464.

7. Jesse Smith, Ledger, 1807–1839.

8. Lang Hall was originally Richard Lang's store from 1791-1820, from 1830-1838 it was the bookstore of Thomas Mann. It is still visible in the right side of the photograph published in the Dartmouth Class Album of 1874. See Notman, William- Photographer. Views used in the Dartmouth Class Albums between 1874-1877 2, Dartmouth College Photographic Files.

9. R. Stuart Wallace, Richard Lang Papers (1791–1825), Finding Aids, New Hampshire Historical Society Manuscripts Division, July 1974.

10. Jesse Smith to Richard Lang, March 25, 1797, Richard Lang Papers, Box 1, Folder 3.

11. Jesse Smith from Richard Lang, 4 February 1799, Tunbridge Deed Book 2:379.

12. Jesse Smith from Benjamin Peabody, 16 December 1799, Tunbridge Deed Book 2:464.

13. Jesse Smith from Amos Allin, 27 November 1799, Tunbridge Deed Book 2:447.

14. Amos Allin from Jesse Smith, 27 November 1799, Tunbridge Deed Book 2:446.

15. Jesse Smith from Benjamin Peabody, 16 December 1799, Tunbridge Deed Book 2:464.

16. Benjamin Peabody from Jesse Smith, 16 December 1799, Tunbridge Deed Book 2:448.

17. John Lasell to Hezekiah Hutchinson, January 31, 1801, Tunbridge Deed Book 2:544.

18. Benjamin Peabody, Account Book, Feb. 7, 1801, Received.

19. John Lasell's headstone is in East Orange in the Hutchinson Cemetery. It can be seen on Find-A-Grave with memorial ID 31676357.

20. Benjamin Peabody, Account Book, March 11, 1802, Recd. Of Jesse Smith.

21. http://www.josephsmithpapers.org/paper-summary/lucy-mack-smith-history-1844-1845/21.

22. Thomas Emerson from Asael Smith, 3 June 1803, Tunbridge Deed Book 3:69. Although Emerson bought the Smith homestead, he clearly did not plan to move there. In 1803 he bought the Archelaus Towne house in Topsfield and moved to Hill Street where he lived until 1828. John H. Towne, "Topsfield Houses and Buildings," *The Historical Collections of the Topsfield Historical Society* (Topsfield, Mass.: Topsfield Historical Society, 1902), 8:21. A witness to his transaction, Billey Emerson, built a brick house on Main Street in Topsfield where he continued to live. Topsfield Historical Society 8:40.

23. Details about Joseph Smith's business activities are explored in detail in another study.

24. Due to space limitations, the details of this business deal will be dealt with in another context.

25. William Adams from Jesse Smith, March 27, 1804, Tunbridge Deed Book 3:138

26. Benjamin Peabody issued a quit claim deed to Jesse Smith for the mortgage on 6 November 1809. Jesse Smith from Benjamin Peabody, 16 November 1809, Tunbridge Deed Book 4:92. Jesse Smith later charged twenty-five dollars to vacate all rights to the property he had earlier sold to the owners of the land in 1810, Samuel Adams, Thomas Barrot, and Alfred Closson. Adams Closson & Barrot from Jesse Smith, 16 November 1810, Tunbridge Deed Book 4:144.

27. James Adams from Asael Smith, 11 October 1805, Tunbridge Deed Book 3:282.

28. Although 266 days before Joseph Smith Jr.'s birth is April 1, 1805, Lucy could have been expecting him anytime from late-March to mid-April.

29. Jesse Smith from Thomas Emerson, 30 September 1805, Quit Claim Mortgage, Tunbridge Deed Book 3:358. Registered in Tunbridge records on 26 March 1806.

30. Benjamin Peabody & Asa How from Jesse Smith, 27 November 1805, Tunbridge Deed Book 3:301. See also, Benjamin Peabody Account Book, Mr Oliver Perkins debits, Mr Eleazu Putnam debits, and Mr Asa How debits.

31. Jesse Smith from Asael Smith, 11 October 1805, Tunbridge Deed Book 3:300.

32. Asael Smith Jun. from Silas Smith, 6 December 1805, Tunbridge Deed Book 3:304.

33. Silas Smith from Asael Smith, 7 December 1805, Tunbridge Deed Book 3:302.

34. Jesse Smith from Silas Smith, 7 December 1805, Tunbridge Deed Book 3:303.

35. Moses D. Rowell from Asael Smith Jun.r, 6 March 1806, Tunbridge Deed Book 3:336.

36. Anderson, *Joseph Smith's New England Heritage*, 143.

37. Anderson, *Joseph Smith's New England Heritage*, 143.

38. Jesse Smith was able to get 90 acres in Lot No 26 for tax and cost with was less than two dollars. The land had belonged to B. Ordway. Jesse Smith, Tax Sale, May 2, 1808, Tunbridge Deed Book 3:537-538. Jesse Smith from Matthew Stanley First Constable, 28 September 1809, Tunbridge Deed Book 4:225. Jesse later sold the property back to the family that settled it for $500. Michael Ordway from Jesse Smith, 24 March 1812, Tunbridge Deed Book 4:228.

39. When Jesse finally sold his 183 acres in Tunbridge to his father-in-law, he did not record the transaction. We don't know when he sold it. But the transfer likely happened years before Peabody sold the property. Peabody transferred the Silas Smith property for $400 to Billey Emerson of Topsfield, a brother of Thomas Emerson, on December 10, 1813. Billey Emerson from Benjamin Peabody, 12 November 1822, Tunbridge Deed Book 5:537. Peabody and How sold lot 10 and lot 17 to Emerson as investments for $1,000. Billey Emerson from Peabody and How, March 21, 1814, Tunbridge Deed Book 5:538. Then Billey Emerson sold to Samuel Bradstreet, also of Topsfield, "two farms situated in Tunbridge" for $733. "The first farm 226 acres is the same farm which I bought of Benjamin Peabody." Emerson then includes details about the original purchase. He acknowledges a joint deed with Benjamin Peabody and Asa How 1 February 1814, Tunbridge Deed Book 5:538. He then acknowledges the second farm of two hundred acres purchased of John Adams in January 1814 "with all the buildings and privileges pertaining to them." This farm included what had become Moxley land, Brewer land, and Dewey land, "and is the same farm which is now cultivated by Sylvanus Brigham & on which the sd. Brigham now lives." Emerson sold the land to Bradstreet for $1,733 to be paid on or before the fourth day of August 1833 registered August 8, 1831.
Adams soon acquired all of Smith settlement, including lot 17 farmland, lot 19 (where Jesse and Hannah Peabody Smith lived), the western half of lot 18 North divided from Joseph and Lucy's property and sold by Asael to younger brother and wife Silas and Ruth Stevens Smith, and lot 10 where Asael and Mary had their frame home, cooper shop, barn, and other structures visible in the 1907 Anderson photographs. Asael sold the west half of Lot 18 North to his son Silas Smith (see Silas Smith from Asael Smith, December 7, 1805, Tunbridge Deed Book 3:302). On the same day Silas then sold the property to his brother Jesse (see Jesse Smith from Silas Smith, December 7, 1805, Tunbridge Deed Book 3:303). Jesse then sold the land to his father-in-law Benjamin Peabody who sold it to Billy Emerson for $400. Peabody was listed as from Middleton, Essex County, Massachusetts and Emerson

was listed as from Topsfield, Essex County, Massachusetts. Billey Emerson from Benjamin Peabody, November 12, 1822, Tunbridge Deed Book 5:537. Billey Emerson purchased lot 10 and lot 17 from Peabody and Asa How. The deed book notes they purchased the 183 acres from Jesse Smith. How is also from Middleton, Essex, Massachusetts, and he and Peabody appear to have invested together and sold their investment to Emerson for $1,000. Billey Emerson from Peabody and How, March 21, 1814, Tunbridge Deed Book 5:538.

40. Adams did not live on the Joseph and Lucy Smith property which limits the numbers and kinds of outbuildings he may have constructed. Adams rented out portions of his land for others to farm, and later when he sold lot 10 in 1848, his deed specifically describes it as "being the farm on which I now live ... with all the privileges and appurtenances there of to." James Adams to John Cowdry, December 1, 1848, Tunbridge Deed Book 6:102, see also the Tunbridge Deed Book for April 1, 1850, 6:167 and January 12, 1852, 6:322 when the land was again described in subsequent transactions to Adams's brother-in-law, Americus K. Howard. James continued to live on lot 10 with his daughter and her husband until his death. The Adams's had houses and barns on three different properties, a large cooper shop big enough to house two families, and more than 360 acres of mountain farmland. They apparently ignored the buildings on their 43 acres in the east half of lot 18 North and let them decay over the years. When property owners in Tunbridge were assessed a tax of one cent per acre on their property April 5, 1813, Moses Davis was assessed a tax for lot 17 and the western half of lot 18 North as the renter of James Adams's property. April 17, 1813, Tunbridge Deed Book 5:540–541. Adams also acquired the Jesse Smith property parcel by parcel beginning with land he acquired through Thomas Moxley. James Adams from Thomas Moxley, October 1, 1815, Tunbridge Deed Book 5:451–452. The history of that land is not reviewed here except to note that Adams acquired another home that appeared as the Lasell home in later nineteenth century township maps. Because the widow of John Lasell was given half of this home, including "the south half of the house ... a privilege of coming & going in & out at the end & back doors & up & down the cellar & chamber stairs & the south half of the cellar & an equal privilege of the dooryard & also a piece of Land beginning at the North East corner of the house thence running northerly on the road four & a half rods to a marked post in the fence ... to cyrus chapman's land ... also the south west scaffold in the barn & west half of the stable under it & one quarter of the yard & a privilvege in the barn of [the] floor" it appears when Adams first acquired the Jesse Smith property he had additional structures on his property—more than he could adequately use—which suggests he did not have a need to build on Joseph and Lucy's property. See John Lasell Estate, May 3, 1831, Tunbridge Deed Book 11:210-211.

Chapter Eight: Lucy's Meadow, Her Grove, and Her First Vision

1. Laurel Thatcher Ulrich, *Good Wives: Image and Reality in the Lives of Women in Northern New England, 1650–1750* (New York: Alfred A. Knopf, 1982), 13.

2. https://www.josephsmithpapers.org/paper-summary/lucy-mack-smith-history-1845/56#full-transcript.

3. Anderson, ed., *Lucy's Book*, 239–240, especially footnote 24.

4. Some historians have suggested Lucy was clerking in Stephen's store when she first met Joseph, see Richard S. Van Wagoner, *Natural Born Seer: Joseph Smith, American Prophet, 1805–1830* (Salt Lake City: Smith-Pettit Foundation, 2016), 9. This interpretation appears to have originated with missionaries at the Joseph Smith Birthplace site in Sharon, Vermont, sometime in the 1980s (see interview notes with Euclid Farnham, October 2016). While Lucy does say "we" when she discusses opening a store with her husband in Randolph in 1802, women were not store clerks. In rare cases they managed a store through their husbands or when inheriting it after the death of their husbands, but these exceptions don't seem to extend to store clerk positions as well. It is likely the role of owner and manager that Lucy had in mind with her use of "we" than a clerking role. Managing a store seems to have been seen as an extension of managing a household and would be the role of the wife of a store keeper and not another woman, see Patricia Cleary, "'She Will be in the Shop': Women's Sphere of Trade in Eighteenth-Century Philadelphia and New York," *The Pennsylvania Magazine of History and Biography* 119, no. 3 (July 1995), 181–202. Laurel Thatcher Ulrich contends "the lives of early American housewives were distinguished less by the tasks they performed than by forms of social organization which linked economic responsibilities to family responsibilities and which tied each woman's household to the larger world of her village or town," Laurel Thatcher Ulrich, *Good Wives: Image and Reality in the Lives of Women in Northern New England, 1650–1750* (New York: Alfred A. Knopf, 1982), 34. In terms of their age, position in the family, and typical roles, Temperance Mack would have been more likely to help her husband manage the store while the younger Lucy cared for the little children at home.

5. Tunbridge Town Records February 22, 1788 and September 9, 1788, 42–43.

6. Tunbridge Town Records March 3, 1791, 52. Tunbridge Town Records June 1, 1791, 59. Child, *Gazetteer of Orange County, Vermont, 1762–1888*, 491.

7. https://www.josephsmithpapers.org/paper-summary/lucy-mack-smith-history-1844-1845/20. See footnote 190 for details about Universalist meeting space.

8. While descendant and family historian Joseph Fielding Smith has attributed his claim the family were Universalists while in Massachusetts to what was "commonly reported in the family," because the family separated themselves from the main religion of the community right after they arrived in Tunbridge, and because they identified themselves as Universalists before the movement became active in Vermont, circumstantial evidence supports Joseph Fielding Smith's claim. See Joseph F. Smith, Jr., "Asahel Smith of Topsfield, with Some Account of the Smith Family," Topsfield Historical Collections (Topsfield, Mass.: Topsfield Historical Society, 1902), 8:89. Tunbridge Town Records February 22, 1788 and September 9, 1788, 42–43. Tunbridge Town Records March 3, 1791, 52. Tunbridge Town Records June 1, 1791, 59. Tunbridge Town Records August 20, 1791, September 6, 1791, 54–55. In addition, the "Mr. Webster" who took the family to Vermont, had to have been a member of the Universalist community since the family was founding members of that movement. Richard Eddy, *Universalism in Gloucester, Mass., An Historical Discourse on the One Hundredth Anniversary of the First Sermon of Rev. John Murray in that Town, Delivered in the Independent Christian Church, November 3, 1874* (Gloucester, Mass.: Procter Brothers, 1892), 188. C. E. Potter, *History of Manchester, formerly Derryfield, in New Hampshire* (Manchester: C.E. Potter, 1856), 220, 234, 258). George Wingate Chase, *The History of Haverhill, Massachusetts, from its First Settlement, in 1640 to the Year 1860* (Haverhill: George Wingate Chase, 1861), 76, 79, 118, 131, 138.

9. Smith family tradition places the family conversion to Universalism in Massachusetts rather than Vermont. Joseph Fielding Smith argued: "It is doubtful if Asael would have again left the place [Topsfield] had he not aroused the prejudices of his neighbors. He was a man of very liberal views, with thoughts in advance of his time. He was noted for having opinions of his own which he would not yield to bigotry nor opposition. Some of his children were baptized in the Congregational church at Topsfield; but in his own religious views he was somewhat of a Universalist.... It is commonly reported in the family that he brought the ill-will of his neighbors upon his head because of his too liberal religious views. It is well known that he was open and explicit and always expressed his honest opinions whether they were in accord with prevailing views or not." Joseph F. Smith, Jr., "Asahel Smith of Topsfield, with Some Account of the Smith Family," Topsfield Historical Collections (Topsfield, Mass.: Topsfield Historical Society, 1902), 8:89. The Tunbridge township records support this tradition as the Smith family immediately distanced themselves from the majority religion in Tunbridge and shortly after their arrival they made their separation formal, see footnote 190 below.

10. Mark W. Harris, "Hosea Ballou's 'Treatise' at 200," UUHS Lecture at General Assembly, Fort Worth, Texas, June 2005, copy in the files of Mark Staker.

11. Although Richard Anderson concluded Asael had a "broad theology" and was apparently sympathetic to the Congregationalists because he purchased a pew in the village meetinghouse (Richard Lloyd Anderson, *Joseph Smith's New England Heritage* (Salt Lake City: Deseret Book, 1971), 207–208, n.183; see also, Anderson, ed., *Lucy's Book*, 291–292, n.24), the township records suggest his purchase of a pew reflects his role as a mediator between the "majority" religion and all the township dissenters. The "majority" religion was considered Presbyterian in the earliest records but later the same congregation and the same minister, David H. Williston, were remembered as Congregationalist. (For a later identification of Williston as Congregational minister see Child, *Gazetteer of Orange County*, 492).

Tunbridge town meetings first focused on religion February 22, 1788, when they discussed the need for a minister and meetinghouse in the main village. This was just over two years before the Smith family arrived. Nothing was accomplished toward an established congregation before the Smith's purchased their property in June 1791. In September 1791, when Jesse and Joseph Smith were on the farm preparing for their family to come, they likely attended the September 6 meeting because the gore where they were settling was the main topic of discussion, and its need for a bridge that would would give the gore's residents access to Jigger village (South Tunbridge) was the issue presented and approved. After its approval, someone raised the issue of religious dissenters and the need to ensure the rights of those that "differ in sentiment" were not infringed. This was the first intimation that not everyone in Tunbridge agreed with the desire to get a minister and build a meetinghouse. During 1793 Asael Smith played a significant role as discussion moderator, selectman assigned to help determine proper placement of the meetinghouse, and leading negotiator of differences over the meetinghouse. He helped bring the community together to "see if everyone can agree on a spot for the meetinghouse." Selling pews for the meetinghouse was a proposal forwarded above Asael Smith's name as a selectman as an alternative to taxing everyone in the community for the building. It gave those without any religious affiliation the ability to opt out of paying for a meetinghouse. He was on a committee of two that negotiated a postponement of construction of the building until they agreed on a location and funding. The community "voted unanimously," one of the few times they did so, to "accept the above report" recommending delay. During the stop construction of the meetinghouse period, the community agreed "all of every denomination in religion & all of every description & character provided they are of age shall be possessed of an equal right in it." Thus anyone who paid for a pew had right to use the building.

Asael was then given the task as a township selectman to see if the town would abate all or part of the tax rates for the poor as thought proper. As part of assessing taxes, those who differed from the Presbyterians in town submitted their names as dissenters. Forty-two men identified themselves as Baptists who did not have a congregation in Tunbridge and were meeting in various locations in neighboring townships. Four did not list a religion. Four were nonattending Catholics tied St. Paul's Church in New Hampshire. One was Episcopalian. And six were part of the Society of Johnsborough that met at the four corners of Tunbridge, Randolph, Bethel, and Royalton.

The ensuing petitions also listed seventeen men who identified themselves as Universalists, including the man who was hired to build the chapel and several who purchased pews in the building. One of the men, Deliverance Brown, later indicated he had never signed the petition and aligned with the Presbyterian majority (see December 6, 1797 and July 10, 1799 entries). It appears that Asael created the petition and may have put the names on of people he considered likeminded. Asael and Jesse Smith and all the other men on the Universal list (or their fathers in some cases) were among the eighty-eight men who signed another petition on November 4, 1794, agreeing that first tax assessed should apply to pew purchases for the building. The men of the town then, "Voted that three Denominations viz. Presbitarians (sic), Universalists and Baptists have Equal Rights in sd. Meeting House on the Sabbath according to the Interest they own in the House." Asael paid eight pounds sterling for his pew and Jesse twelve pounds. Their purchase of pews did not reflect an interest in the Congregationalists or Presbyterians, but it helped pay for Universalist access to the building where they could meet. Hosea Ballou undoubtedly preached in the Tunbridge meetinghouse when he came through the area. "Tunbridge Proprietors Book: Containing the Proceedings of Proprietors of said Tunbridge Attested by Elias Curtis Proprietors Clerk AD 1785," Tunbridge Clerk's Office, Tunbridge, Vermont, 42–43, 54–55, 59, 82, 87–88, 91–94, 185–189, 195–208, 245.

There has been some confusion among historians because of the signature of a Joseph Smith in the township records identifying himself as an "Anabaptist," "Tunbridge Proprietors Book," 443, (see Dan Vogel, ed., *Early Mormon Documents* (Salt Lake City: Signature Books, 1996), 1:636–637). The record was filled out by local town clerk Hezekiah Hutchinson as part of a large packet of records submitted by Chelsea Township clerk David Crocker. Chelsea is the township on the northern border of Tunbridge. All of Crocker's petitions were for those attending the Baptist congregation in Chelsea, and in the petition Hutchinson included, he noted the signees were "separate from all other Denominations Except those called by the Name or Appelation of Anabaptists." He did not say they belonged to the Anabaptists. It is clear the Hutchinson's petition was part of the larger packet of Crocker petitions. It was completed November 12, 1799, but it was recorded in 1802 along with the other Chelsea Baptist records completed over several years. There were many Baptists in the area, but there was not an Anabaptist congregation. The other Joseph Smith who married Hannah Fifield and lived in Tunbridge on the northern border convenient to the Chelsea congregation was likely a Baptist. Crocker filled out a separate petition for his brother, Stephen Smith, earlier that same year (see June 10, 1799 Petition, Tunbridge Proprietors Book, 188; for their relationship see,

Child, *Gazetteer of Orange County, Vermont, 1762–1888*, 344). The Chelsea Baptist congregation was too far away for Joseph Smith who was the son of Mary and Asael Smith to conveniently attend, and Lucy makes it clear in her narrative that her husband only attended the Methodist meetings with her because she desired it. https://www.josephsmithpapers.org/paper-summary/lucy-mack-smith-history-1845/55.

12. For details on the conflict between the Tunbridge Congregationalists, Presbyterians, Baptists, and Universalists, including Asael Smith's role in that controversy, see continual entries in the Tunbridge Township, Tunbridge Minute Book, beginning in 1790 on page 59 and continuing through the rest of the eighteenth century. See especially pages 180–188 which includes the list of Tunbridge Township residents who did not want to pay taxes to support the "majority" religion, i.e. David Williston's Congregationalists. Asael Smith presented a list of residents recorded on page 188 who had already formed themselves "into a society [that] wish[ed] to be known by the Name or forme of universalists" and did not want to be taxed to support Williston's group. The Universalist list was recorded on December 6, 1797. But this list, like the rest of the entries in this section of the minutes, was included to address the issue of taxes for a church and minister, not to organize a congregation. Many others—mostly Baptists but some in other denominations—also registered with the township expressing their differences with "the majority." The Universalists did not need to provide a list of members to the township to hold meetings, and Universalists had been meeting in nearby townships as early as 1792. Asael Smith was the moderator for the township who arranged for the list, and his name appears second on the list underneath Alexander Stedman (while his sons Jesse and Joseph appear apart later in the list). But it is not clear who made the list or if it was done by consent. Deliverance Brown asked two years later that his name be removed from the list and noted it was included without his approval. No one else had their name removed.

13. Maturin M. Ballou, *Biography of Rev. Hosea Ballou, by His Youngest Son* (Boston: Abel Tompkins, 1852), 64–88.

14. Ballou identifies himself on the title page of his influential theology as the "Ordained Pastor of the United Societies of Barnard, Woodstock, Hartland, Bethel and Bridgewater." Hosea Ballou, *A Treatise on Atonement; in which, the Finite Nature of Sin is Argued, Its Cause and Consequences as Such; the Necessity and Nature of Atonement; and its Glorious Consequences, in the Final Reconciliation of All Men to Holiness and Happiness* (Randolph, Vermont: Sereno Wright, 1805), Title Page. Little is known of his congregations in the neighboring townships, and he does not include Tunbridge or East Randolph on his list. But Ballou wrote of traveling rough roads in the area by horseback to preach to remote congregations. He sometimes preached in areas where there was not an established congregation including as far away as Utica. His son also remembered he covered a "large field" when going

from congregation to congregation. Ballou, *Biography of Rev. Hosea Ballou, 75, 79, 89.* Since someone was preaching in East Randolph during Ballou's travels, and he was in the area, it is likely he was the one doing that.

15. Edith Fox MacDonald, *Rebellion in the Mountains: The Story of Universalism and Unitarianism in Vermont* (Concord, New Hampshire: The New Hampshire Vermont District of the Unitarian Universalist Association, 1976), 75; and Nickerson & Cox, arr. And comp., *The Illustrated Historical Souvenir of Randolph, Vermont,* 28.

16. Child, *Gazetteer of Orange County, Vermont, 1762–1888,* 344.

17. Hosea Ballou, *A Treatise on Atonement: in which, the finite nature of sin is argued, its cause and consequences as such; the necessity and nature of atonement; and its glorious consequences, in the final reconciliation of all men to holiness and happiness* (Randolph, Vermont: Sereno Wright, 1805). Sereno Wright lived from 1779–1858 and became the printer for Vermont state publications. He married Fanny Carpenter on October 19, 1803, Vermont Vital Records, 1720–1908, (1870 and prior). Most if not all of the preaching in Randolph Township took place in East Randolph during the first few decades of settlement and congregations in Randolph Center and West Randolph were not even established until after Joseph and Lucy Smith had moved to western New York, see Homer White, *History of the Church in Randolph, Vermont* (West Randolph, Vermont: Herald, 1885), 1–2, 4.

18. For the influence on Ballou, see "Ethan Allen: Reason, the Only Oracle of Man, 1784," in, Dan McKanan, ed., *A Documentary History of Unitarian Universalism, from the Beginning to 1899* (Boston: Skinner House Books, 2017), 101–102.

19. Oscar Safford, *Hosea Ballou: A Marvelous Life Story* (Boston: Universlist Publishing House, 1889), 74. John E. Remsburg, *Thomas Paine: The Apostle of Liberty* (New York: The Truth Seeker Co., 1917), 108. Ernest Cassara, *Hosea Ballou, Preacher of Universal Salvation,* Boston University Thesis, 1957, 57, 133.

20. Benjamin Kolenda, "Re-Discovering Ethan Allen and Thomas Young's Reason the Only Oracle of Man: The Rise of Deism in PreRevolutionary America," Thesis, Georgia State University, 2013, 47.

21. McKanan, "Ethan Allen: Reason, the Only Oracle of Man, 1784," 101. Ethan Allen, *Reason, The Only Oracle of Man: or a Compenduous (sic) System of Natural Religion* (Bennington, Vermont: Haswell & Russell, 1784), 57.

22. Allen, *Reason, The Only Oracle of Man* 106–108. See also, Ethan Allen to Royall Tyler, Letter August 28, 1787, John J. Duffy, ed., *Ethan Allen and His Kin, Correspon-*

dence, 1772–1819: A Selected Edition in Two Volumes (Hanover: University Press of New England, 1998), 245.

23. Thomas Paine, *Common Sense: Addressed to the Inhabitants of America*, (Philadelphia: R. Bell, 1776), N.p.

24. Thomas Paine, The Age of Reason (part II) originally published in 1795. The third section of Paine's *Age of Reason*, where he would begin to distance himself from Christianity as a whole, would not be printed until 1807, after Joseph Smith had begun to distance himself from Paine's writings.

25. Hosea Ballou, *A Treatise on Atonement; in which, the Finite Nature of Sin is Argued, Its Cause and Consequences as Such; the Necessity and Nature of Atonement; and its Glorious Consequences, in the Final Reconciliation of All Men to Holiness and Happiness* (Randolph, Vermont: Sereno Wright, 1805), iv.

26. John Murray, "Records of the Life of the Rev. John Murray, 1816," Dan McKanan, ed., *A Documentary History of Unitarian Universalism: From the Beginning to 1899* (Boston: Skinner House Books, 2017), 154–159. Caleb Rich, "Narrative of Elder Caleb Rich," McKanan, ed., *A Documentary History of Unitarian Universalism*, 209. Universalists developed an article of faith in 1790 that the Holy Ghost spoke to people through the scriptures, see "Philadelphia Convention of Universalists 'Articles of Faith and Plan of Church Government' 1790," McKanan, ed., *A Documentary History of Unitarian Universalism*, 120.

27. Hosea Ballou, *A Treatise on Atonement; in which, the Finite Nature of Sin is Argued, Its Cause and Consequences as Such; the Necessity and Nature of Atonement; and its Glorious Consequences, in the Final Reconciliation of All Men to Holiness and Happiness* (Randolph, Vermont: Sereno Wright, 1805), 171, 181. Ballou acknowledged some of his readers might experience "feeling some disagreeable emotion" when reading his work, but he dismisses that emotional response and appealed to ration and finding "saving knowledge."

28. Asael Smith, "My Dear Selfs, Letter, April 10, 1799," Archives and Library, The Church of Jesus Christ of Latter-day Saints, MS 1139. Digital copy available online at: https://dcms.lds.org/delivery/DeliveryManagerServlet?dps_pid=IE4753063. Although the letter was catalogued noting it was not clear if it was a copy or the original, Asael Smith's signature at the end of the letter is identical to the Asael Smith signature on the deed of property transfer from Asael to Silas Smith in Tunbridge, Vermont. See Asael Smith to Silas Smith, 6 December 1805, Tunbridge Deed Book, 3:302.

29. Ballou, *A Treatise on Atonement*, 104–105, and Peter Hughes, "Hosea Ballou," in McKanan, ed., *A Documentary History of Unitarian Universalism*, 136.

30. For an introduction to Shouting Methodists, see Mark Staker, *Hearken, O Ye People: The Historical Setting of Joseph Smith's Ohio Revelations* (Salt Lake City: Greg Kofford Books, 2009), 125–139.

31. Newton, "History of the Old Barnard Circuit," 1917, 104–105.

32. William M. Newton, "When Vermont Methodism First Saw Her Bishop or Asbury in Vermont," 1917, 2, 4, 6, 9, 13, William Monroe Newton, Manuscript History Collection, Boston University School of Theology. Newton, "History of the Barnard Circuit," 1917, 2–4.

33. Newton, "History of the Old Barnard Circuit," 1917, 106, 108.

34. Child, *Gazetteer of Orange County, Vermont, 1762–1888*, 492, places the organization of a Methodist congregation in South Tunbridge village to "about 1810," and construction of their "first house of worship," to 1833. But a room still survives above the barn of a home just north of the old brick church where early class meetings were held around 1810 or earlier. The hinges, door handles, and other features in the room are consistent with a ca. 1810 period furnishing. We took extensive photographs and measurements of this room and have placed them on file in the Historic Sites Division files of the Church History Library in Salt Lake City. It is possible Joseph and Lucy attended early class meetings in this structure. But we don't know where they first attended.

35. Joseph Dix, ed., *Letters, Containing Some Account of the Work of God Since the Year 1800* (Barnard, Vt.: I. H. Carpenter, Printer, 1812), 6, 15–17.

36. Figures are based on adding up the total numbers of people in each column. The total written in the original document included a math error and is not correct. U. S. Census, Vershire, Vermont, 1800.

37. Child, *Gazetteer of Orange County, Vermont, 1762–1888*, 344.

38. Dix, ed., *Letters*, 6, 15–17.

39. Hannah Allen to Jane Addams of "chalcey" [Chelsea], Vermont. Undated, MSS SC 2449, Special Collections, Brigham Young University. Although this letter is dated 1810 in the BYU Special Collections catalog, the date is probably assigned because that was the year Tunbridge first organized its own Methodist branch. Hannah Allen was a contemporary of Lucy Smith, but her granddaughter Jane Allen Addams

was born in Chelsea September 8, 1813. Several of the other Tunbridge women Allen mentions (such as Caroline Howe Fuller, born 1814), also date to after 1810. It is likely Hannah Allen is referring to a revival sometime in the 1830s. But the Methodist experience is identical and the context similar to that of the earlier enthusiasm. Her point that the Lord had left them suggests a cooling off period during the 1820s.

40. Dix, ed., *Letters*, 6, 15–17.

41. Elleanor Knight, *A Narrative of the Christian Experiences, Life and Adventures, Trials and Labours of Elleanor Knight, Written by Herself* (Providence, R.I.: Knight, 1839), 88.

42. Dix, ed., *Letters*, 6, 18.

43. Dix, ed., *Letters*, 52.

44. Anne P. Wheeler, "The Music of the Early Nineteenth-Century Camp Meeting: Song in Service to Evangelistic Revival," *Methodist History* 48, no. 1 (October 2009), 26.

45. Enoch Mudge, *The American Camp-Meeting Hymn Book: Containing a Variety of Original Hymns, Suitable to be Used at Camp-Meetings; and at Other Times in Private and Social Devotion*, 1818, 143-45.

46. Emily C. Blackman, *History of Susquehanna County, Pennsylvania* (Philadelphia: Claxton, Remsen and Haffelfinger, 1873), 138.

47. Rev. Lyman Potter, "Records of the First Congregational Church in Randolph Vermont May 30th 1786 to December 30th 1831," pp.29–49. Microfilm copy available at the Kimball Library, Randolph, Vermont.

48. Potter, "Records of the First Congregational Church in Randolph Vermont May 30th 1786 to December 30th 1831," 68.

49. https://www.josephsmithpapers.org/paper-summary/lucy-mack-smith-history-1844-1845/21. It is clear Lucy was uncertain about his name after so many years as the additional references to him were of a "Mr. M." John Moxley is the only individual in the entire township who has a name like the one Lucy used. See Randolph, US Census, 1800.

50. Child, *Gazetteer of Orange County, Vermont, 1762–1888*, 344.

51. Lucy Mack Smith History, 1845, 48. https://www.josephsmithpapers.org/paper-summary/lucy-mack-smith-history-1845/55.

52. Lucy Mack Smith History, 1845, 48. https://www.josephsmithpapers.org/paper-summary/lucy-mack-smith-history-1845/55.

53. https://www.josephsmithpapers.org/paper-summary/lucy-mack-smith-history-1845/56#full-transcript

54. Lavina Fielding Anderson, "Mother Tongue: King James Version Language in Smith Family Discourse," Mormon History Association, 2009.

55. Deacon Experience Davis died December 14, 1809, at age 77. Buried in the East Bethel Cemetery settlers erected a monument for him that reads: "The first settler of Randolph—an honest man & friend of humanity. Erected by the town of Randolph in 1860 as a memorial of his liberal bequest for the support of schools in Randolph." For additional details, including his residence in East Randolph on the southeast side of the road and information about his adopted son, Jacob Annis, see "Last Will and Testament of Experience Davis of Randolph, 19 January 1803," Randolph Township Records, Deed Book 12 January 1810, 4:509–510. Experience Davis to Wollcott Allyn fifty acres of land, 20 December 1802, Randolph Town Records1802–1806, Deeds, 3:30. Experience Davis to Peter Walker, Randolph Town Deeds, 1:80. Experience Davis to David Green, November 29, 1785. Randolph Town Records 1783–1797, Deeds, 1:190. Experience Davis to Nathan Davis, 24 October 1784, Randolph Town Records 1783–1797, Deeds, 1:192. see also Timothy Miles to Cornelius Russell, 4 November 1794, Randolph Town Records 1783–1797, Deeds, 1: 435–436, and Experience Davis to Thomas Gowin, 2 November 1793, Randolph Town Records1783–1797, Deed Book, 1:455.

56. G. Walter Fiske, "A Page of Methods: A Grist of Questions from Country Churches," *The Congregationalist and Christian World* 92, no. 42 (17 October 1908), 502-503.

57. https://www.josephsmithpapers.org/paper-summary/lucy-mack-smith-history-1845/56#full-transcript

58. https://www.josephsmithpapers.org/paper-summary/lucy-mack-smith-history-1845/56#full-transcript

59. Anderson, ed., *Lucy's Book*, 291.

60. Anderson, ed., *Lucy's Book*, 292. For details about black cherry trees in relation to operating a dairy, see notes of conversations with Vermont dairyman Jerry Kill, August 2017, in Mark Staker's files.

61. George A. Smith placed the baby's birth to 1797 but did not give a specific day. There is some confusion in the sources as to its gender with some evidence suggesting it was a girl and some evidence suggesting a boy. See, Anderson, ed., *Lucy's Book*, 264, n.101.

62. https://www.josephsmithpapers.org/paper-summary/lucy-mack-smith-history-1844-1845/245

63. There is some evidence in the manuscript that Lucy and her scribe Martha Coray are drawing from a first-person manuscript written by Joseph Smith Sr. in retelling the dreams. If so, this would suggest he gave them great weight and attempted to preserve their content himself, see Sharalyn D. Howcroft, "A Textual and Archival Reexamination of Lucy Mack Smith's History," in Mark Ashurst-McGee, Robin Scott Jensen, and Sharalyn D. Howcroft, eds., *Foundational Texts of Mormonism: Examining Major Early Sources* (New York: Oxford University Press, 2018), 324.

64. The earliest surviving manuscript versions of Joseph Sr.'s dreams were recorded in Lucy's narrative where she likened the Book of Mormon to her own circumstances. She compared her travels to Kirtland, Ohio, with the journey made by "father Lehi." Anderson, ed., *Lucy's Book*, 514. Howcroft, "Lucy Mack Smith's History," 312. Each of her husband's dreams included elements that reflected similarities to Lehi's dream which he had while making that journey. It appears Lucy continued the comparison throughout the narrative and not only likened herself to Lehi but likened her husband to Lehi. When the manuscripts containing the dreams were later moved into the Vermont part of the narrative, Lucy's attempt to pattern her experiences on those in the Book of Mormon was lost. Lavina Fielding Anderson, who edited *Lucy's Book*, acknowledges this change in ordering when she notes she followed the order Coray gave the dream in her later 1845 manuscript and in the Coray/Pratt 1853 version of the history, see Anderson, *Lucy's Book*, 295. Sharalyn Howcroft had kept the original ordering in the Joseph Smith Papers version of the manuscript at https://www.josephsmithpapers.org/paper-summary/lucy-mack-smith-history-1844-1845/245.

65. Anderson, ed., *Lucy's Book*, 298.

Joseph and Lucy Smith's Tunbridge Farm

Index

Adams, James, 53, 55
Adams, William, 53, 54, 55
Allen, Ethan, 59–60, 64
Allen, Hannah, 62
Allin, Amos, 51
Apple varieties, 13

Ballou, Hosea, 58–60, 66
Barnard Twp., Vt., 59, 61
Bethel Twp., Vt., 13, 62, 63
Bill, Lydia Mack, 18
Bill, Samuel, 18
Buck, Isaac, 11

Cider, 20, 44, 47
Clinton, George, 4
Cooper shop, 46, 48
Creamware ceramics, 38–41
Curtis, Elias, 58

Davis, Experience, 5, 66
Durkee, Heman, 10

Emerson, Thomas, 53
Gilsum, N. H., 18, 35–36
Ginseng, 44, 47
Green Mountains, 1
Grow, Peter, 58

Hannover, N. H., 51
Hops (and Oast), 20–22, 44, 47
Houghton, Richard, 4
How, Asa, 54
Howard, Americus K., 55
Howard, Jane Adams, 55
Hutchinson, John, 6

Ipswich, Mass., 1

Lang, Richard, 19, 51
Lasell, James, 52, 53
Log cabin/house, 23–25, 27–34

Manchester, N. Y., 8
Marsh, Joel, 5, 10
Mack, Lovina, 57–58, 69
Mack, Lovisa, 57–58, 69
Mack, Lydia, 69
Mack, Stephen, 18, 36, 52, 57
Mack Temperance, 36, 57
Methodists, 52, 61–66, 68, 69
Moxley, John, 52, 53, 64–65
Moxley, Laura E. Lasell, 52, 53
Moxley, Thomas, 52
Mudget, John, 36,
Murray, John, 60

Nails, 29, 45

Orange County, Vt., 62
Paine, Thomas, 59–60, 65
Palmyra, N. Y., 20
Peabody, Benjamin, 25, 26, 37, 39, 49–50, 53, 54
Peabody, Joseph, 50
Pearlware ceramics, 41–43, 45
Potsdam, N. Y., 55

Queensware ceramics, 38–39

Randolph Congregational Church, 64
Randolph Twp., Vt. (East Randolph village), 5, 21, 59, 61, 62, 64
Rowell, Moses D., 54
Royalton, 4–7, 5, 6, 53, 61
Rum, 39-40

Sharon Twp., Vt., 36, 53, 54, 61
Smith, Alvin, 27
Smith, Asael, 1, 6, 8, 9, 10, 14, 16, 17, 26, 27, 38, 40, 48, 49, 53, 54, 55
Smith, Asael, Jr., 53, 54
Smith, Benjamin Peabody, 55
Smith, Hannah Peabody, 16, 25
Smith, Jesse, 10, 13, 14, 16, 19, 24–26, 37, 40, 50, 54, 68
Smith, John, 23, 28–29
Smith, Joseph, Sr., 1, 13, 14, 16, 19, 23–28, 35, 48, 49, 53, 64, 68–69
Smith, Lucy Mack, 1, 13, 18–19, 23, 26–28, 35, 39, 42, 48, 49, 53, 56–69
Smith, Mary Duty, 1, 10, 14, 16, 17, 31, 37, 38, 39, 40, 42, 48, 49
Smith, Mary (Polly), 10
Smith, Priscilla, 10, 13, 25
Smith, Robert, 8
Smith, Ruth Stevens, 55
Smith, Samuel, Jr., 8
Smith, Samuel, Sr., 8
Smith, Sarah, 10
Smith, Silas, 53, 54, 55

Smith, Susannah, 10
Smith Settlement, 1, 2, 18, 48–55, 56
Stevens, Elias, 4, 5, 6, 7, 8–9, 10

Towne, Jacob, Jr., 26, 40
Tracy, Elijah, 24–25, 27, 33
Tunbridge Twp., Vt., 5, 6
Tunbridge Gore, 5, 6, 58
Tunbridge Mountain, 1, 7
Tunbridge villages, 27
Tyler, Mary Palmer, 35
Tyler, Royall, 35

Universalists, 58–62, 64, 68–70

Valentine, Thomas, 5

Waller, Daniel, 13
Waller, David, 5, 7
Ward Hill Meadow, 7
Ward Hill Road, 27
White River, 7
Whittingham, John, 8
Williams, Silas, 6
Williston, David H., 58, 64
Windsor County, Vt., 4

About the Authors

Mark L. Staker

Mark Staker is a Master Curator in the Historic Sites Division of The Church of Jesus Christ of Latter-day Saints. He holds a doctorate in anthropology from the University of Florida. He has spent twenty-seven years developing museum exhibits and researching, restoring or reconstructing, and furnishing buildings for historic sites central to the history of Mormonism. His best-known work includes the restored Priesthood Restoration Site of 1820s Harmony, Pennsylvania and Historic Kirtland Village of 1830s Kirtland, Ohio.

Donald L. Enders

Don Enders is a retired Master Curator in the Historic Sites Division of The Church of Jesus Christ of Latter-day Saints. He holds two master's degrees, one in archaeology and the other in history, both from Brigham Young University. He has spent fifty-five years working to understand the physical setting of Mormonism, starting with excavations at the Nauvoo Temple site in 1965, and including archaeology at the Smith family Palmyra log home site and physical studies of the surviving Smith family Manchester home and the E.B. Grandin Palmyra printshop.

www.ingramcontent.com/pod-product-compliance
Lightning Source LLC
LaVergne TN
LVHW051844080426
835512LV00018B/3058